SPELLING

WEEKLY PRACTICE

ACTIVITY WORKBOOK

This book belongs to

Cover designed by Aiden Anderson
and Noah Anderson

Hi there,
Welcome to your amazing spelling workbook! Get ready for a fantastic adventure with words!

Each week, you'll have eight special words to explore and conquer. These words are like magical treasures waiting for you to discover them. Are you excited? I know I am!

Your workbook is your very own spell castle. You'll find four fun activities for each of your eight words every week. It's like having a secret code to unlock the magic of spelling!

I believe in you and can't wait for you to conquer first-grade spelling!

Remember to;
- **Complete each activity weekly**
- **Say the words**
- **And more importantly, have fun and celebrate your progress**

Happy spelling,

We would love to hear from you!

Email us at kendypress@gmail.com or simply scan the code below.

We will send some free stuff your way!

TABLE OF CONTENTS

TRACE AND WRITE

Say and trace the word.   Write each word (2) two times.

the   the   the

of

and

a

cat

mat

sat

hat

I CAN SPELL

Circle the correct word to match the picture.

Circle the correct spelling of the word.

a   the   and   of

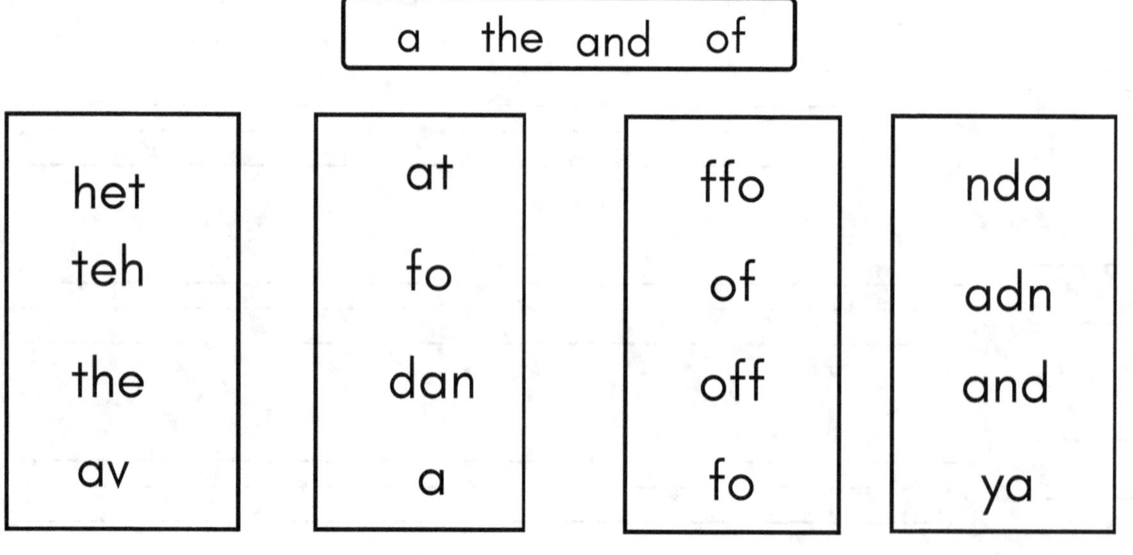

FILL IN THE BLANKS

Read the sentence. Fill in the blank with the correct word from below.

a	mat	cat	and
hat	of	the	sat

1. My pet is a _________________ .

2. _________________ sun is bright.

3. I have a red _________________ .

4. She _________________ on the chair.

5. Tim _________________ Andy are best friends.

6. _________________ all my friends Tom is the best.

7. The dog sat on the _________________ .

8. _________________ frog jumped in the pond.

Name:

Class:

WEEK 1

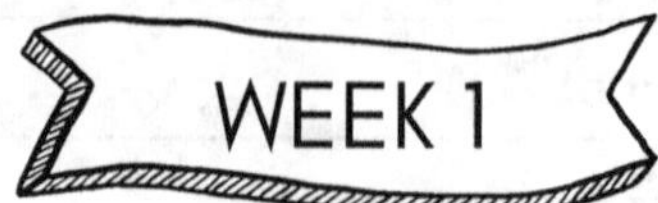

MATCHING

Draw a line to match the words.

and	a
a	mat
sat	and
of	the
cat	sat
mat	hat
the	of
hat	cat

TRACE AND WRITE

Say and trace the word.   Write each word (2) two times.

to

in

is

you

can

man

pan

ran

WORD SEARCH

Find and circle the words. Say and check the words that you find.

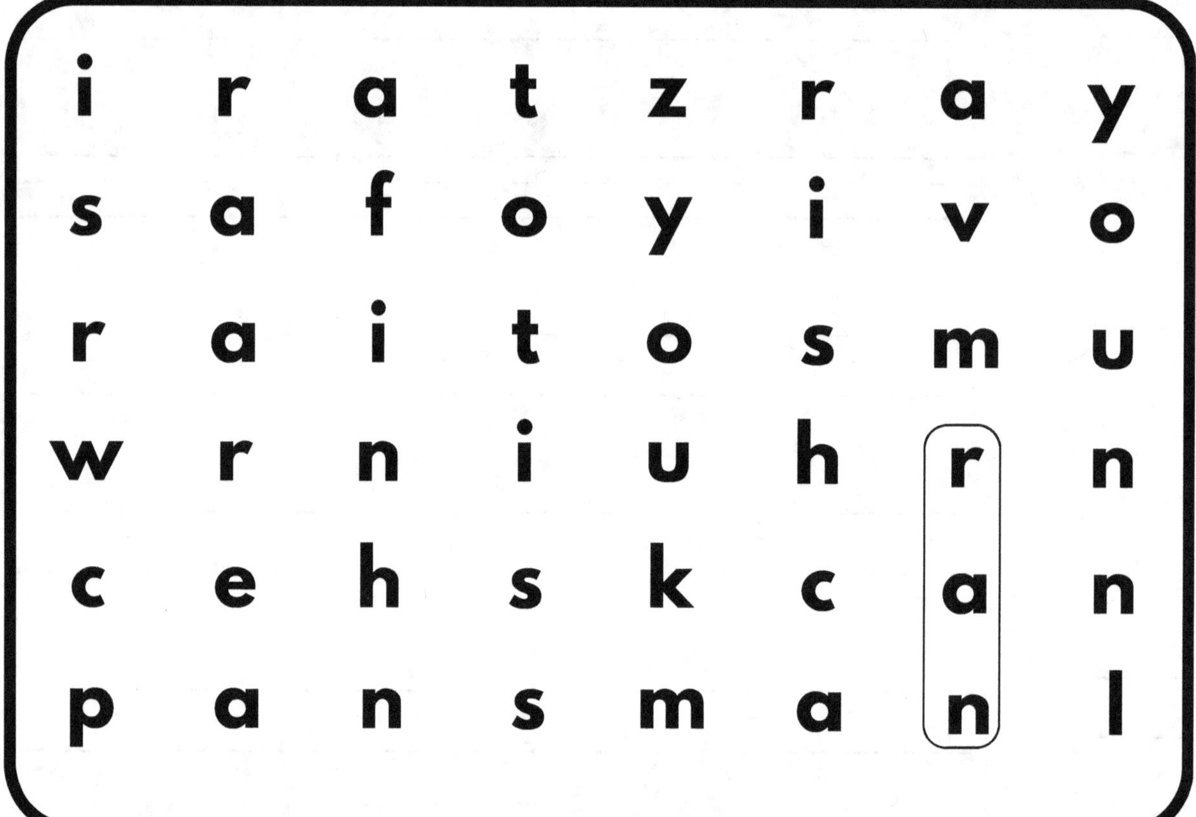

6

COMPLETE THE WORD

Choose a letter from the balloons to complete the word below.

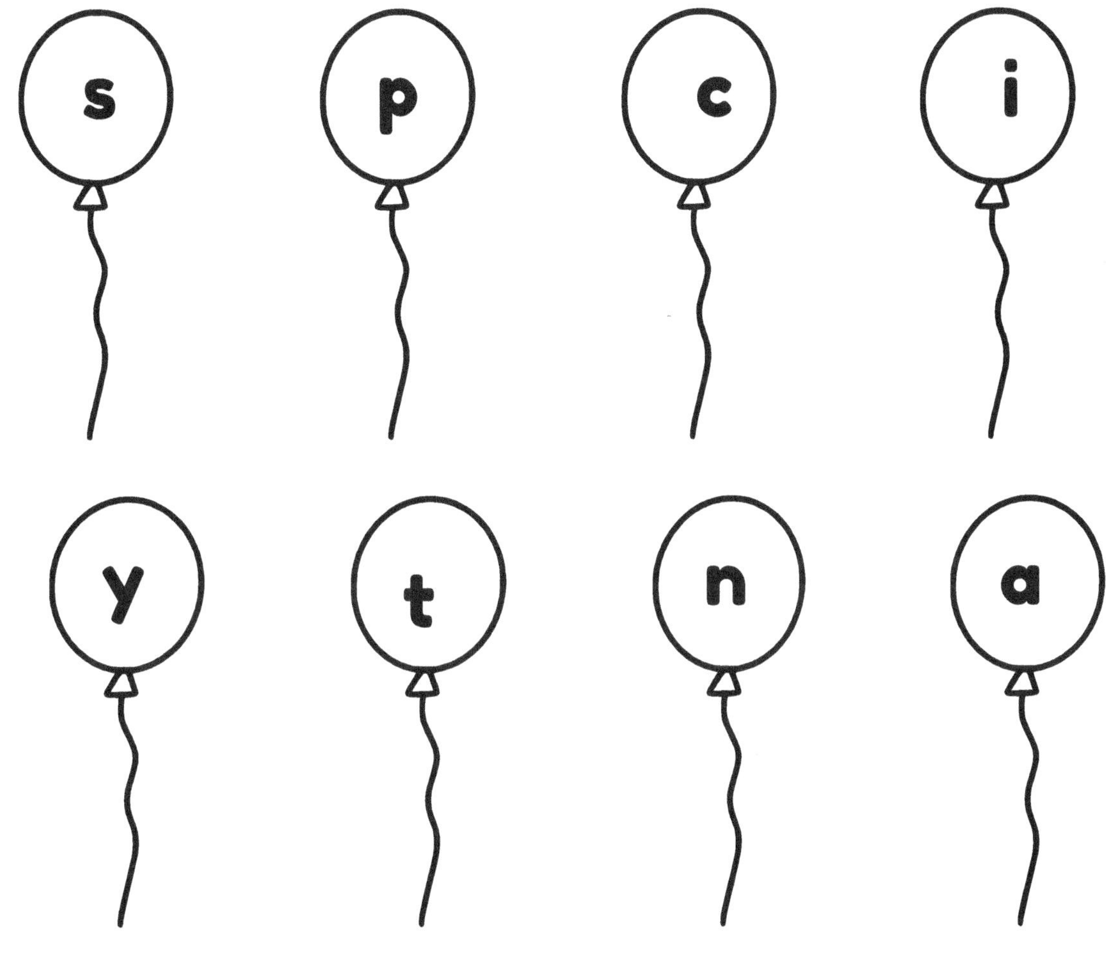

_ ou   m a _   i _   _ o

_ an   _ n   _ an   r _ n

FIND THE WORDS

Read the passage and circle the words.

pan	**is**	**can**	**to**
man	**in**	**you**	**ran**

My name is Justin.

I ran all the way to school.

On m way to school, I saw a man with a pan in his hand.

Can you tell this was fun?

TRACE AND WRITE

Say and trace the word.   Write each word (2) two times.

that

it

he

was

map

cap

nap

tap

WORD SEARCH

Find and circle the words. Say and check the words that you find.

t	h	a	t	a	p
w	e	l	e	g	k
a	i	p	i	f	m
s	a	p	t	i	a
n	i	n	c	a	p

tap	was	map	it
nap	cap	he	that

Name:

Class:

WEEK 3

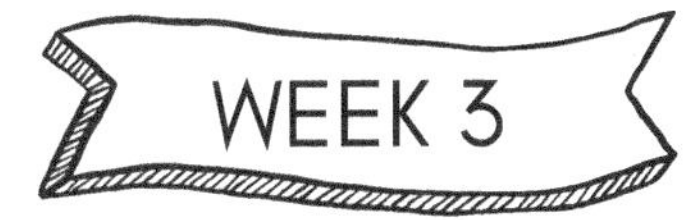

SPELLING TREE

Color the correct spelling of the words in the apple tree.

tap	was	map	it
nap	cap	he	that

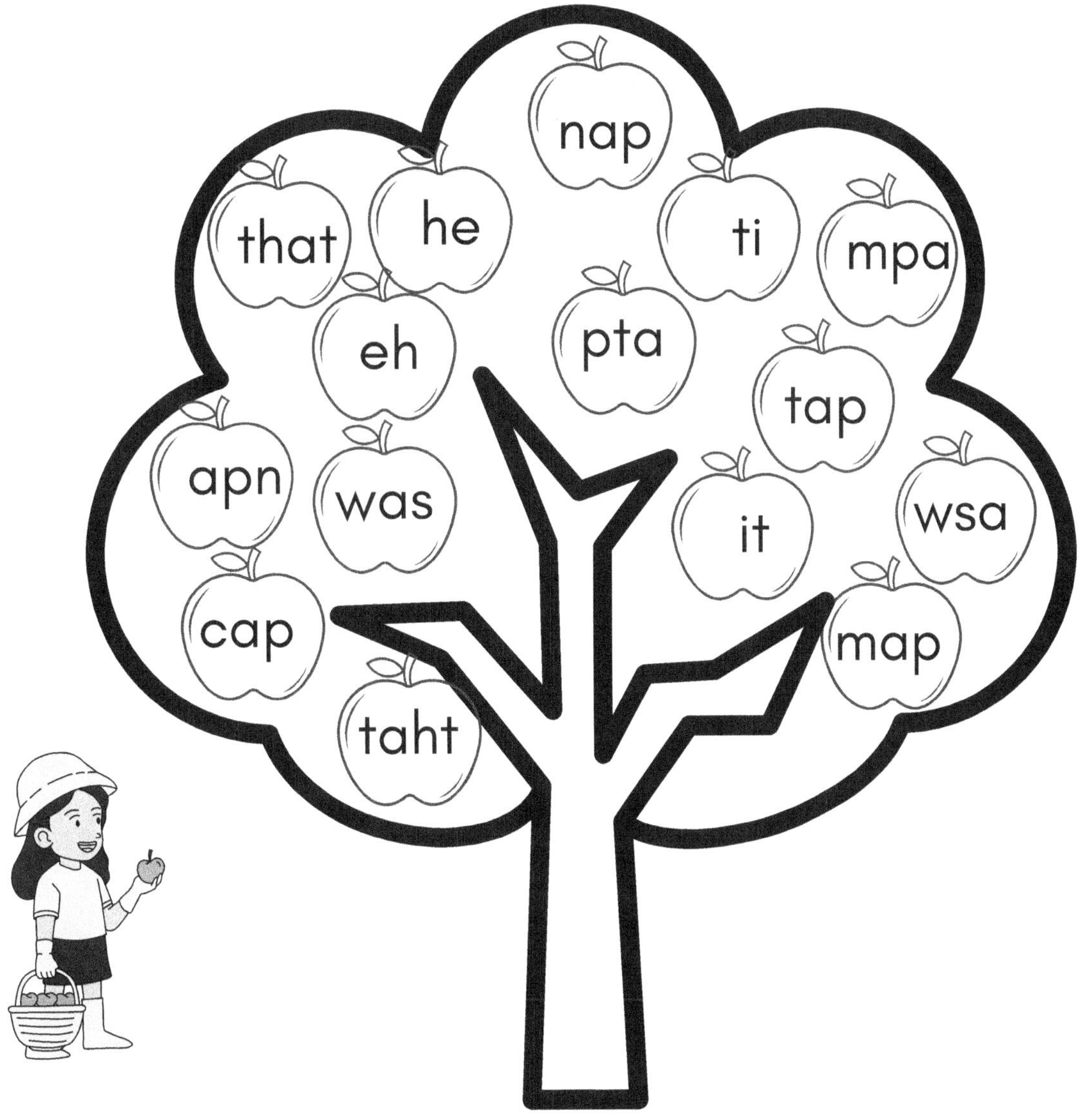

Name:

Class:

WEEK 3

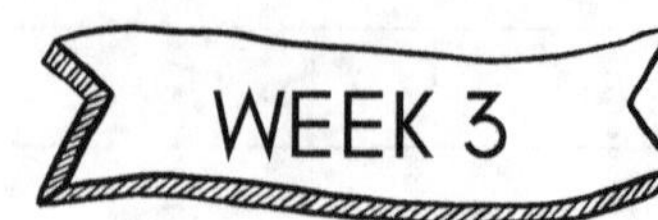

BUILD A WORD

Connect the given letters to build the word.

t •	• ap
c •	• as
m •	• ap
t •	• e
n •	• ap
i •	• hat
h •	• t
w •	• ap

TRACE AND WRITE

Say and trace the word.   Write each word (2) two times.

for

on

are

as

back

sack

black

snack

COMPLETE THE SENTENCES

Read the sentence. Choose the correct word from the list to complete the sentence.

> for   sack   as   on
>
> snack   black are back

1. Who a _ e you?

2. I went f _ r a walk.

3. The frog was _ n the bench.

4. She put her hat in the _ a c k .

5. An apple makes a yummy _ n a c k .

6. She dressed up _ s a bee.

7. Are you _ a c k?

8. Mary wore her _ l a c k dress.

Name:

Class:

CROSSWORD

Follow the numbers and fill in the crossword grid with the correct words.

Down

1. black
3. on
4. sack
6. are

Across

2. as
4. snack
5. back
7. for

Name:

Class:

WEEK 4

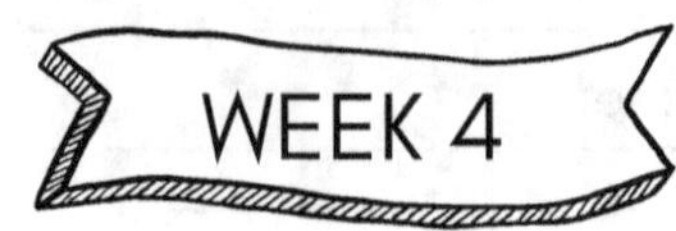

FIND THE WORDS

Color the hearts with the correctly spelled words.

snack as on

sa back are ackb

acks rof for

kbkc black sncka rea

rae sack cblak

TRACE AND WRITE

Say and trace the word.   Write each word (2) two times.

with

his

fit

bit

I

sack

they

sit

COLOR THE WORDS

Say and color the words.

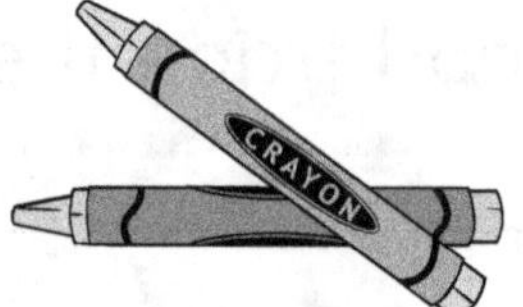

I sit they

with fit

bit his hit

WORD SEARCH

Find and circle the words. Say and check the words that you find.

t	s	i	t	a	h
h	i	t	i	g	i
e	i	h	f	f	s
y	a	i	b	i	t
w	i	t	h	t	t

I	his	bit	they
with	fit	hit	sit

WRITE THE WORD

Look at the picture and complete the word.

Color the letters for the word and write the word in the box.

| h | x | o | i | l | v | k | s | f |
| a | g | b | n | i | g | y | t | s |

Fill in the letter to complete the word in the sentence.

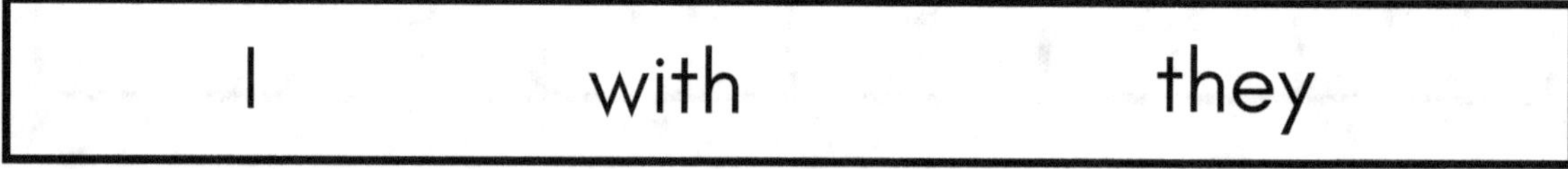

1. Can I come _ith you?

2. _ am happy.

3. _hey are my friends.

TRACE AND WRITE

Say and trace the word.   Write each word (2) two times.

at

be

this

have

big

pig

dig

wig

SPELL THE WORD

Fill in the letters and complete the word to match the pictures.

_ig   _ig   _ig   _ig

Circle the correct spelling of the word.

| at | be | this | have |

tee	re	thes	heav
ta	be	tsih	hvea
at	eeb	thsi	have
mt	eb	this	aveh

Name:

Class:

WEEK 6

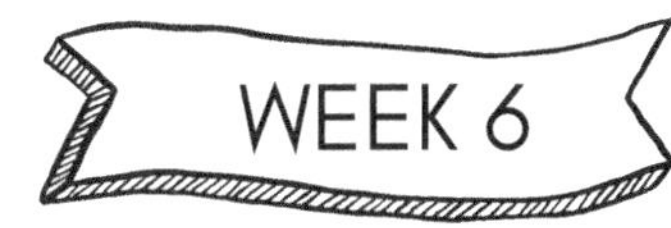

BUILD A WORD

Connect the given letters to build the word.

b •	• ig
a •	• ave
w •	• e
b •	• ig
d •	• his
p •	• ig
h •	• t
t •	• ig

Name:

Class:

WEEK 6

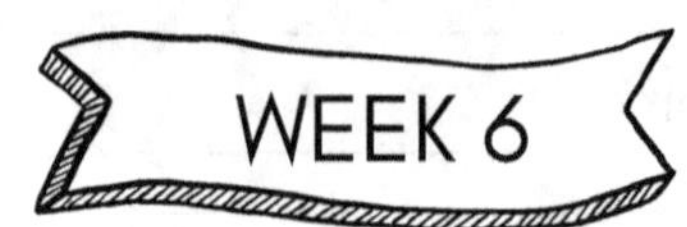

FIND THE WORDS

Tom the frog needs your help! Help Tom circle all the correctly spelled words in his pond.

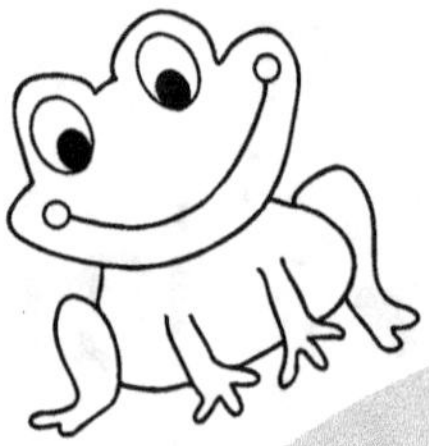

pig be idg igp

be haev have

have wig

at

isth this

eb

ta dig this

igb

at

big

TRACE AND WRITE

Say and trace the word.   Write each word (2) two times.

from

or

one

had

pin

thin

spin

skin

SPELL THE WORD

Look at the picture and write the word.

Color the letters to spell the word.

thin	t	z	c	h	c	i	g	n
from	b	f	t	r	g	o	h	m
had	c	h	o	c	a	g	d	u
or	b	y	o	d	g	r	t	g

MATCHING

Draw lines to match the words.

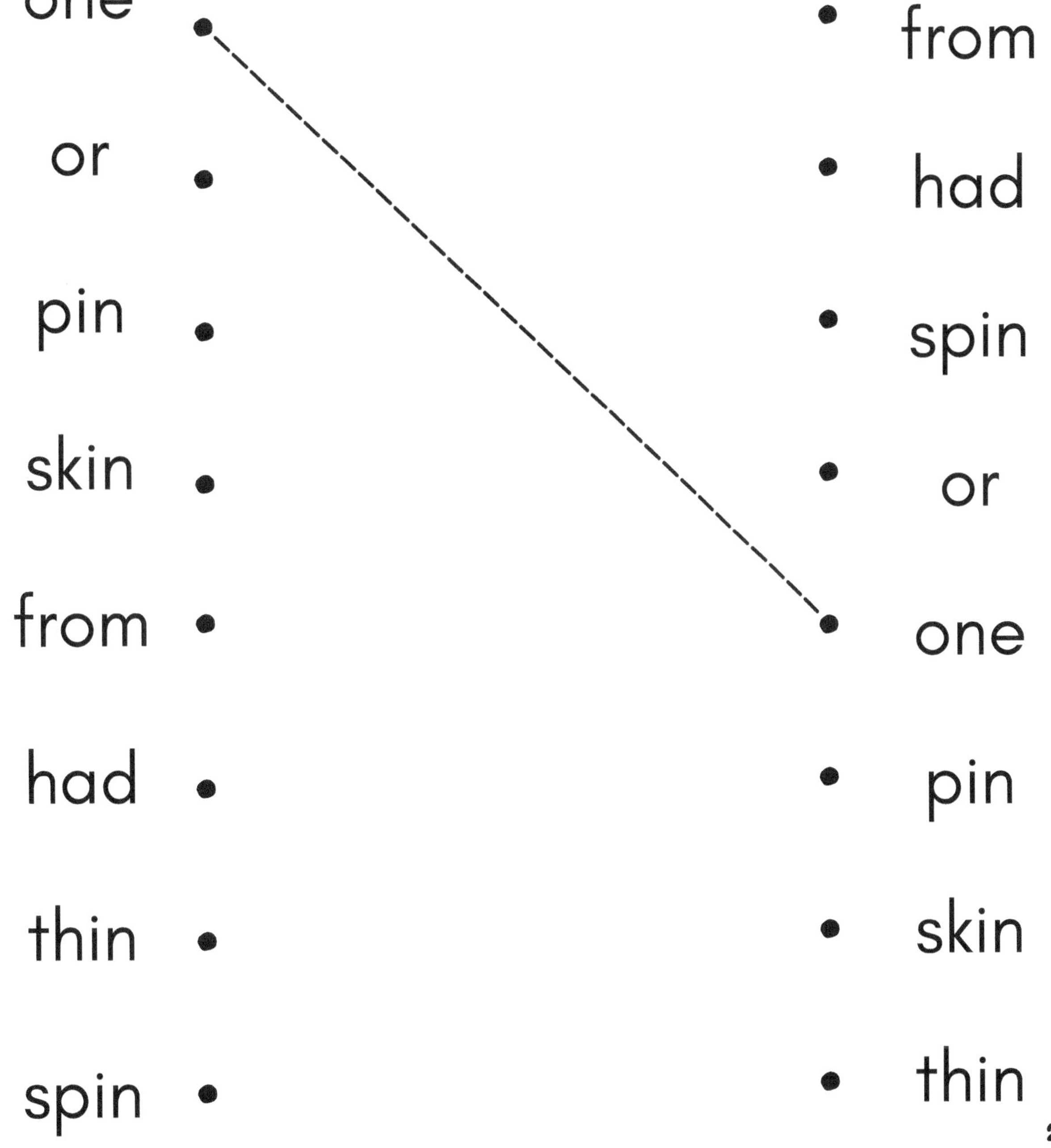

COLOR THE WORD

Say and color the words.

pin thin or

skin from

one had fit

TRACE AND WRITE

Say and trace the word.   Write each word (2) two times.

by

words

but

not

sick

kick

brick

stick

I CAN SPELL

Color the circles with the correctly spelled words.

nto	words	brick	sikc	brikc
yb	not	stick	tbu	kick
by	but	stkic	sick	ikck

Write the word on the lines.

SPELL THE WORD

Look at the picture and circle the correct word.

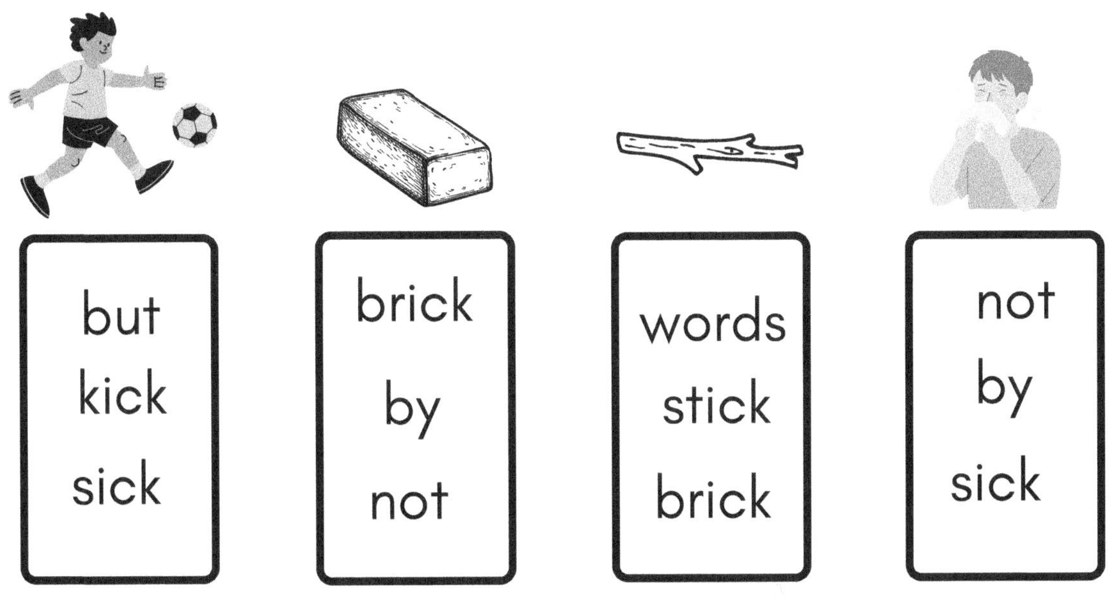

Color the correctly spelled words.

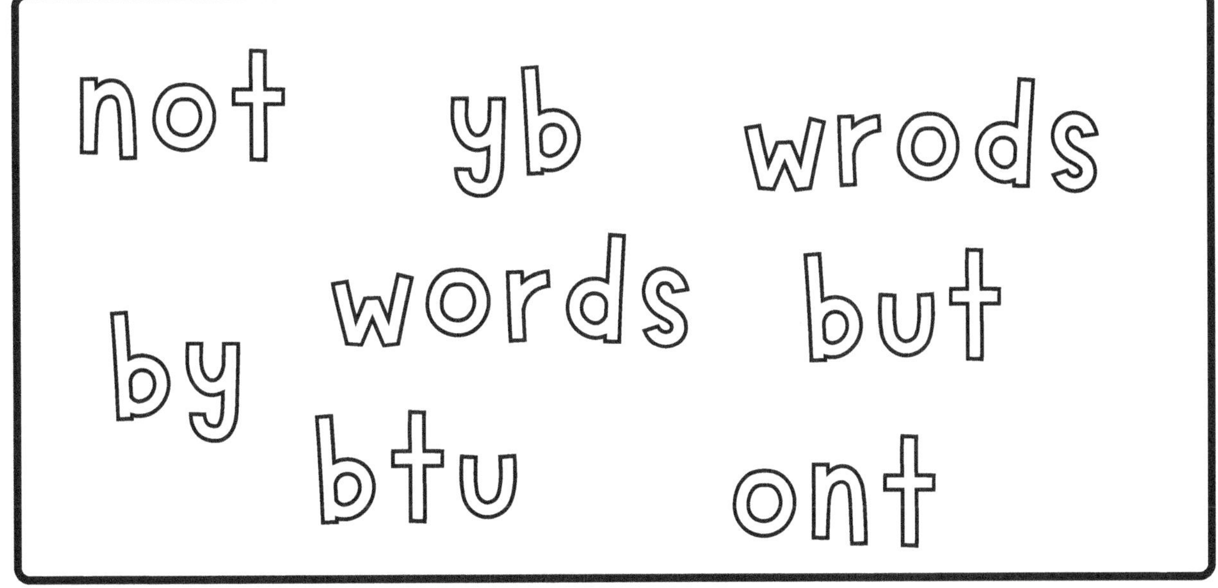

WORD SEARCH

Find and circle the words. Say and check the words that you find.

S	I	C	K	M	M	Y	L	B
T	H	A	I	R	O	A	Y	R
I	O	F	C	O	O	L	K	I
C	I	I	K	C	N	I	N	C
K	E	T	C	C	O	Y	O	K
F	R	F	B	U	T	S	O	H
W	O	R	D	S	O	B	Y	A

by	not	stick	words
but	sick	kick	brick

TRACE AND WRITE

Say and trace the word.   Write each word (2) two times.

what

all

were

we

hot

pot

not

lot

COMPLETE THE SENTENCE

Complete the sentences with the words below.

what	were	we	hot
pot	not	all	lot

The p_t is h_t.

My dog barks a l_t.

wh_t do you think?

A_l my socks are gray.

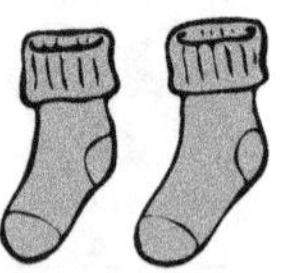

W_ we_e happy.

BEAR FISHING

Bernie the bear is fishing. Help Bernie by circling the correctly spelled words.

WORD SEARCH

Find and circle the words. Say and check the words that you find.

W	H	A	T	L	V	Y	H
E	O	L	R	O	F	O	O
R	S	L	O	T	P	O	T
E	T	O	P	D	H	R	N
I	N	Y	D	N	O	U	O
W	E	E	N	O	P	S	T
R	M	O	P	T	E	G	Y

what	were	we	hot
pot	not	all	lot

TRACE AND WRITE

Say and trace the word.   Write each word (2) two times.

when

your

can

said

mop

top

hop

drop

I CAN SPELL

Look at the picture and fill in the letter to complete the word.

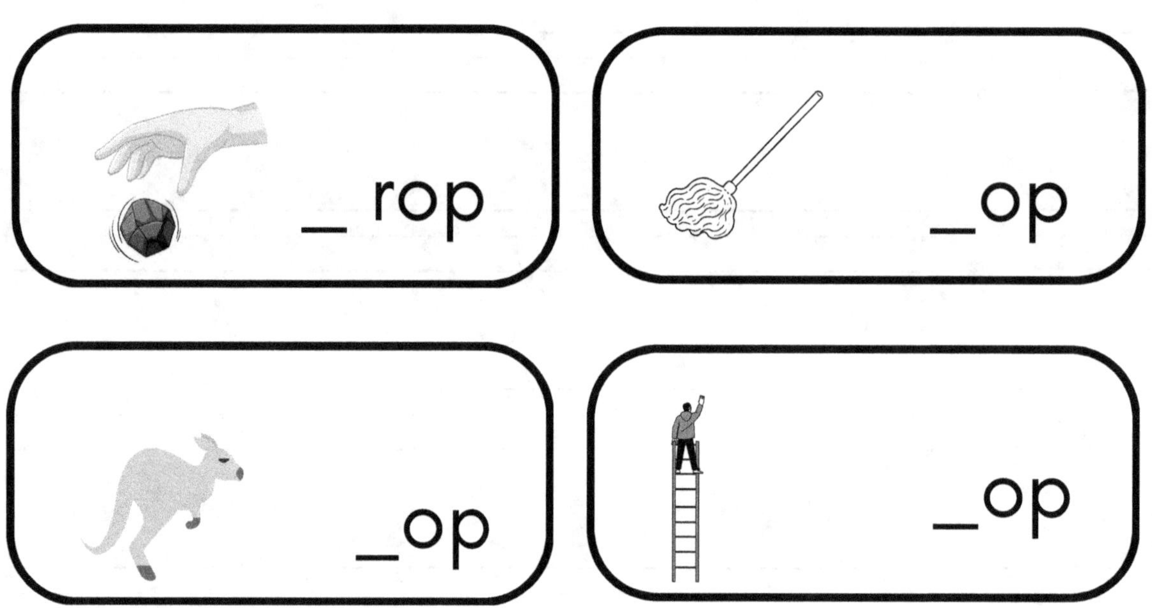

Color the apples with the correctly spelled words.

WORD SEARCH

Find and circle the words. Say and check the words that you find.

```
S   A   I   D   H   V   Y   H
R   O   K   R   A   F   O   C
L   S   U   O   N   Y   U   A
O   T   O   P   D   H   R   N
I   N   Y   D   Y   O   U   R
W   H   E   N   N   P   S   D
R   M   O   P   R   E   G   Y
```

mop	hop	drop	top
when	can	said	your

FIND THE WORD

Use the words below to complete the sentences.
Write the word on the line.

can	drop	top	hop
when	mop	your	said

1. She ———————— jump high.

2. ———————— is your game? 

3. The ————————is wet. 

4. Who is ————————teacher?

5. I like to ———————— like a bunny. 

6. A ———————— of water fell. 

7. I have a spinning ————————.

8.. Who ———————— fishing is not fun? 

TRACE AND WRITE

Say and trace the word.   Write each word (2) two times.

there

use

an

each

job

mob

cob

rob

READ AND SPELL

Circle the word that is spelled correctly in each row.

an	na	aan	an
use	use	ues	sue
each	echa	each	ceah
cob	rob	cob	bco
there	three	trehe	there
job	bjo	job	jbo
rob	rbo	rob	orb
mob	mbo	mob	bmo

BUILD A WORD

Use the letters below to build the words.

u   t   e   o   o
o   n   o

m b

a

c b

ach

j b

here

r b

se

Name:

Class:

WEEK 11

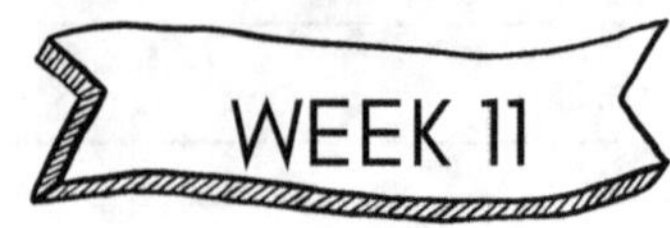

MATCHING

Draw lines to match the words.

cob	rob
mob	there
use	each
job	an
each	use
rob	cob
there	mob
an	job

TRACE AND WRITE

Say and trace the word.   Write each word (2) two times.

which

she

do

how

sock

rock

block

clock

COLORING

Color the words.

she

which

rock

clock

how

do

sock

block

Name:

Class:

FIND THE WORD

Use the words below to complete the sentences.

do	she	rock	sock
how	which	clock	block

1. ——————— are you?

2. ——————— is a great dancer.

3. I ——————— love my cat?

4. My ——————— is wet.

5. I went ——————— climbing .

6. The ——————— is at noon.

7. A ——————— of ice fell.

BUILD A WORD

Connect the given letters to build the word. Then write each word on the lines.

d	how	__________
r	she	__________
s	block	__________
w	do	__do__
h	sock	__________
c	rock	__________
b	clock	__________
s	which	__________

TRACE AND WRITE

Say and trace the word.   Write each word (2) two times.

there

if

will

up

cut

but

hut

shut

FIND THE WORD

Circle the correct word to match each picture.

uth

hut

htu

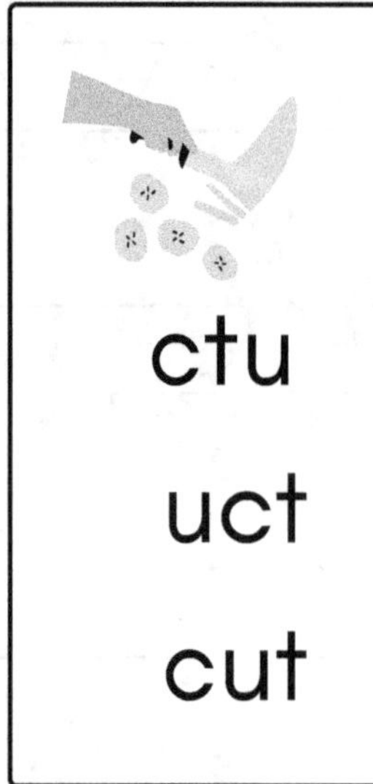

ctu

uct

cut

stuh

shut

huts

pu

pi

up

Read the sentence below. Complete the sentence with the correct word.

| if | but | will | their |

1. ______________ pet is a dog.

2. I ______________ go with you.

3. He jumped ______________ did not fall.

4. I do not mind ______________ it rains.

COMPLETE THE WORD

Color the letter to complete the word. Write the letter on the line to complete the word.

| up   shut   if   cut   but   hut   will   their |

(p)(b)(z)

——ut

(p)(y)(c)

——ut

(j)(b)(i)

——— ill

(i)(g)(k)

——— f

(a)(t)(i)

——heir

(i)(m)(s)

——hut

(y)(g)(p)

——— p

(l)(h)(j)

——— ut

Name:

Class:

COLORING

Say and color the words.

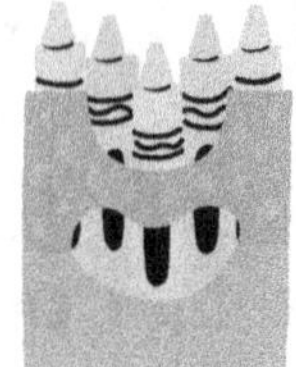

if

up

their

will

cut

hut

but

shut

TRACE AND WRITE

Say and trace the word.   Write each word (2) two times.

other

about

out

many

bug

hug

rug

mug

I CAN SPELL

Say what the picture is then write the letter on the blank to complete the word.

h_g

b_g

m_g

r_g

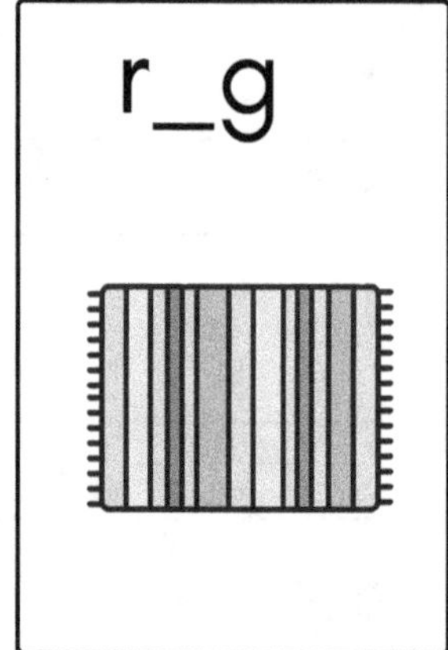

m_any

Circle the words that are spelled correctly.

out   othre   boaut

other   otu   tou

ohter   tabou   about

Name:

Class:

MATCHING

Draw a line to match the letter to the correct words.

b

h

o

o

r

m

a

rug

bug

about

mug

other

out

out

BUILD A WORD

Say the words below. Then fill in the missing letters on the blank to complete the word.

out	other	bug	rug
many	about	hug	mug

m _ g   b _ g

_ o t   a _ t

h _ g   m _ y

r _ g   _ o r

TRACE AND WRITE

Say and trace the word.   Write each word (2) two times.

then

them

these

so

fun

sun

run

bun

FIND THE CORRECT WORD

Find and color all the words that are spelled correctly.

run

os

tehm

unr

these

thme

teshe

unb

rnu

thsee

unf

uns

bun

nfu

then

oso

fun

snu

hten

ubu

so

them

hent

sun

MATCHING

Draw a line to match the words.

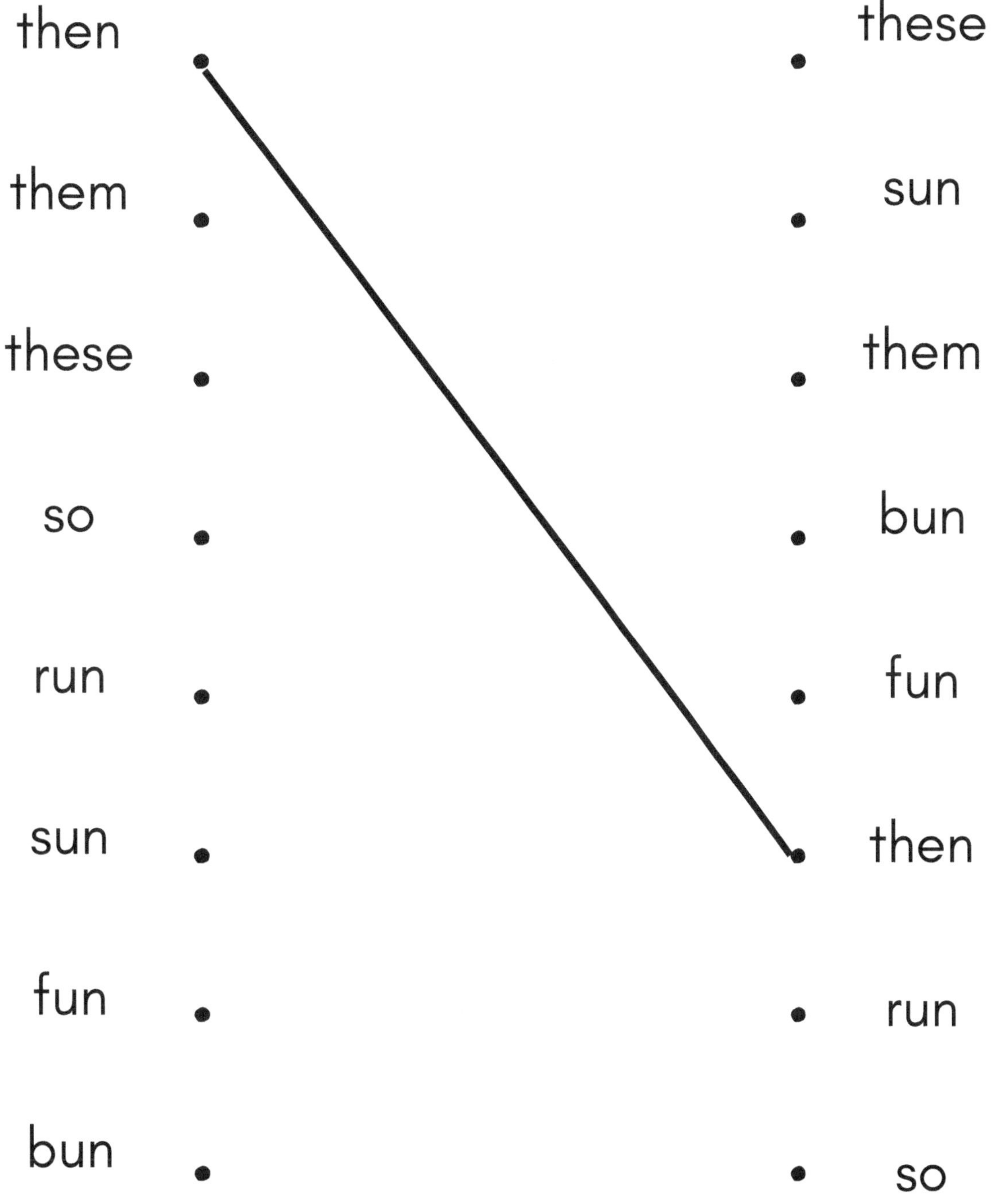

WORD SEARCH

Find and circle the words. Say and check the words that you find.

F	J	T	H	E	M	
U	O	K	H	A	F	
N	S	B	E	N	T	
O	T	U	S	S	H	
R	U	N	E	O	E	
S	U	N	N	N	N	

sun	these	so	then
fun	bun	run	them

TRACE AND WRITE

Say and trace the word.   Write each word (2) two times.

some

her

would

make

duck

luck

suck

stuck

FIND THE WORD

Circle the word that is spelled correctly in each set.

msoe some osme	ehr erh her	wuldo would wuold	akem mkea make
duck uckd dkuc	uckl luck lcku	sukc suck ucks	stuck sutck stcuk

CROSSWORD

Follow the numbers and fill in the crossword grid with the correct words.

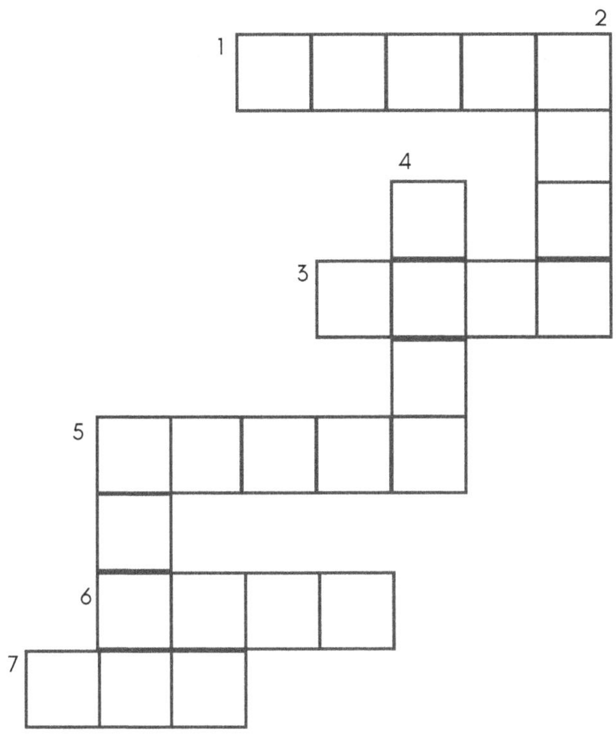

Across

1. would

3. suck

5. stuck

6. make

7. her

Down

2. duck

4. luck

5. some

THE MISSING LETTER

Say the words below and write the missing letter on the blank to complete the word.

stuck	make	duck	would
some	luck	her	suck

wo_ld

m_ke

d_ck

l_ck

s_me

st_ck

h_r

s_ck

TRACE AND WRITE

Say and trace the word.   Write each word (2) two times.

like

into

time

him

pet

get

wet

let

COMPLETE THE WORD

Say the words below and write the missing letter on the blank to complete the word.

> let into time like
> pet wet him get

ti_e   i_to

p_t   l_ck

w_t   g_t

l_t   h_m

FIND THE WORD

Circle the correct word to match each picture.

kile
ilek
like

tle
etl
let

imh
him
ihm

wet
etw
tew

pet
pte
tpe

iton
into
ntio

time
itme
temi

egt
get
egt

Name:

Class:

WEEK 17

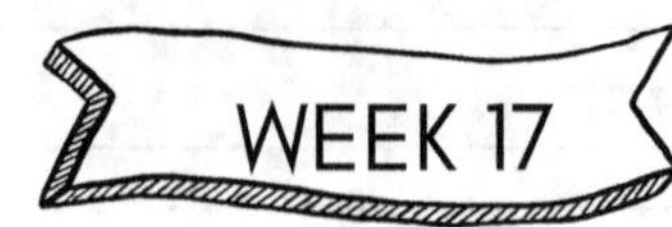

MATCHING

Draw a line to match the words.

like	him
pet	get
into	time
him	like
get	let
wet	pet
time	into
let	wet

TRACE AND WRITE

Say and trace the word.   Write each word (2) two times.

has

look

two

more

fed

bed

red

sled

COLORING

Say and color the words.

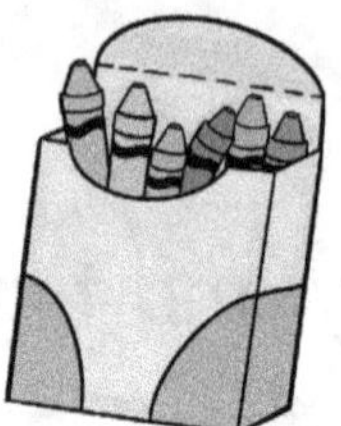

has

red

look

sled

fed

two

bed

more

FIND THE WORD.

Say the words below. Read the sentences and circle the words.

look	two	fed	bed
has	red	sled	more

1. She has a red sled.

2. Did you look at more toys?

3. We fed two ducks.

4. They went to bed early.

COMPLETE THE WORD

Say the words below and write the missing letter on the blank to complete the word.

look	two	fed	bed
has	red	sled	more

sl_d

f_d

h_s

r_d

t_o

lo_k

d_d

mo_e

TRACE AND WRITE

Say and trace the word.   Write each word (2) two times.

write

go

see

number

men

hen

ten

pen

Name:

Class:

WEEK 19

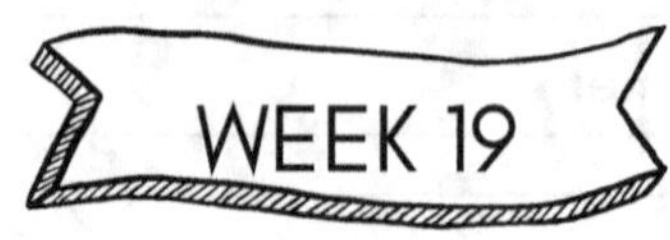

COMPLETE THE WORD

Say the words below and write the missing letter on the blank to complete the word.

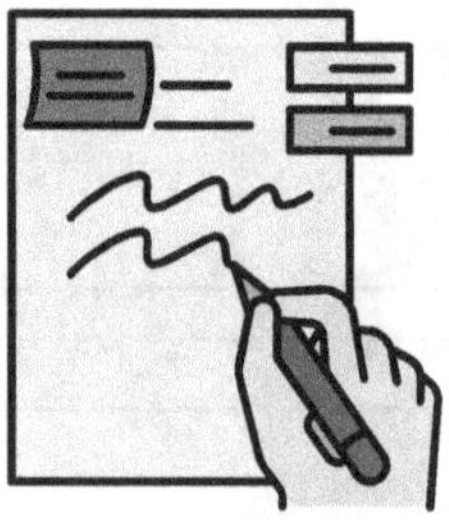

_rite

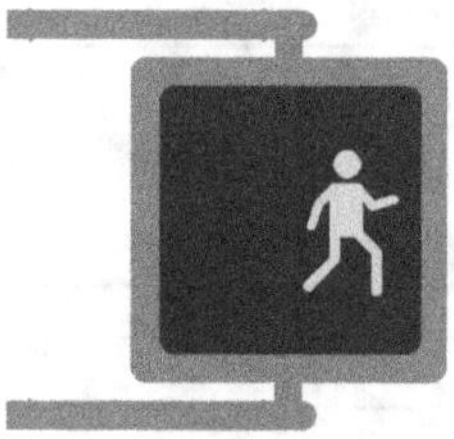

_o

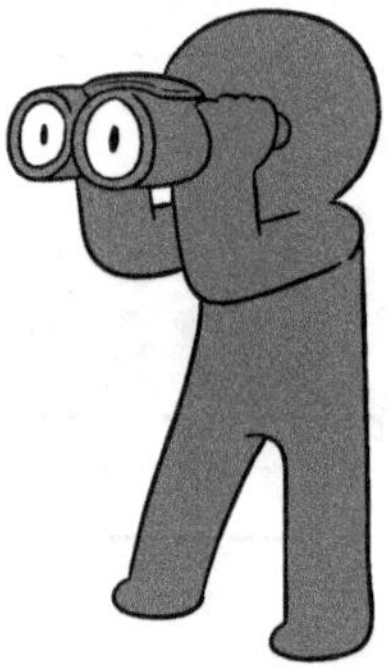

_ee

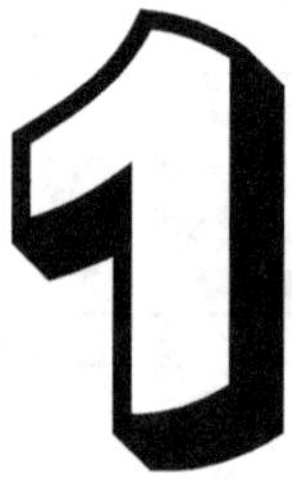

_umber

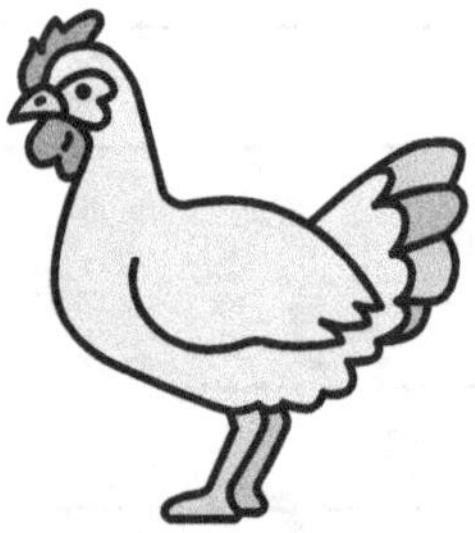

_en

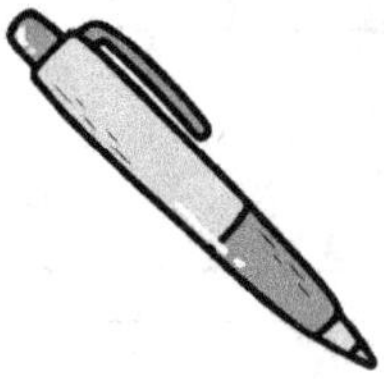

_en

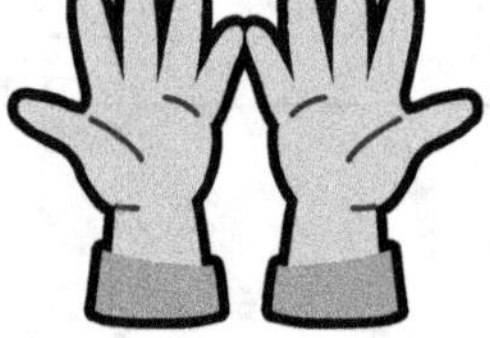

_en

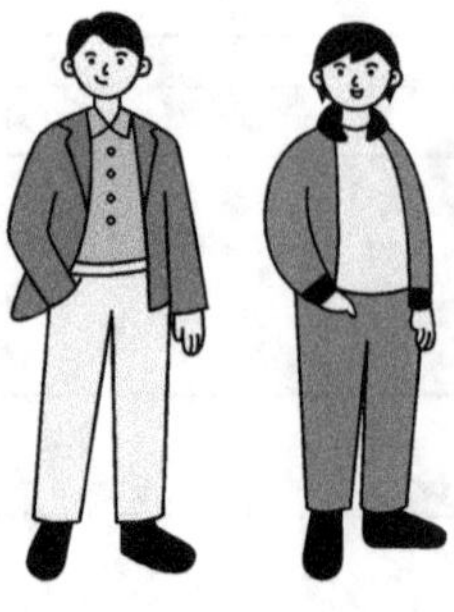

_en

Name:

Class:

WEEK 19

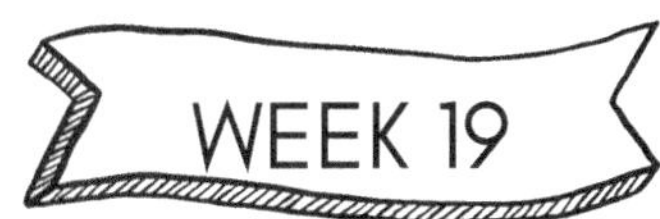

MATCHING

Draw a line to match the word with the correct picture.

see	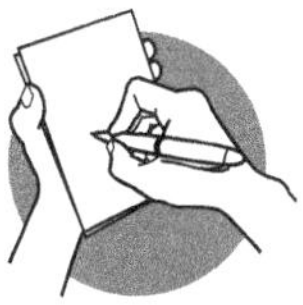
number	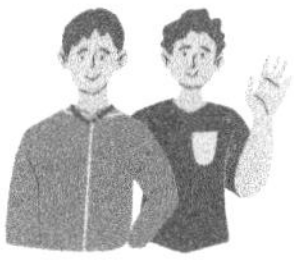
go	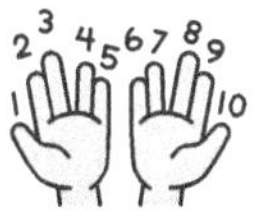
write	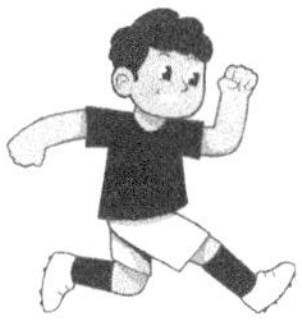
hen	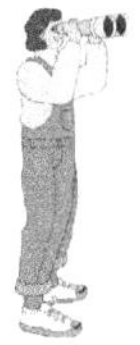
ten	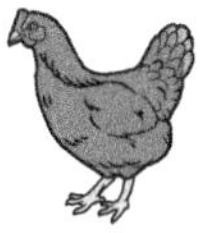
pen	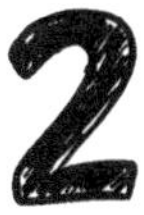
men	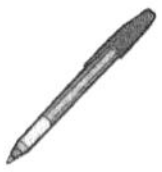

FIND THE WORD

Circle the correct word to match each picture.

ten
ent
net

enm
nem
men

nmbuer
nubemr
number

epn
pen
enp

nhe
enh
hen

ees
see
ese

ogo
og
go

rwite
write
rtwie

TRACE AND WRITE

Say and trace the word.   Write each word (2) two times.

no

way

could

people

tell

well

sell

fell

FIND THE WORD

Color the correctly spelled word in each set.

on	ouldc	wya	wlel
no	culod	way	ellw
oon	could	ayw	well

peolep	ltel	flel	sell
people	tlel	fell	slel
peploe	tell	ellf	slel

Name:

Class:

MATCHING

Draw a line to match the words.

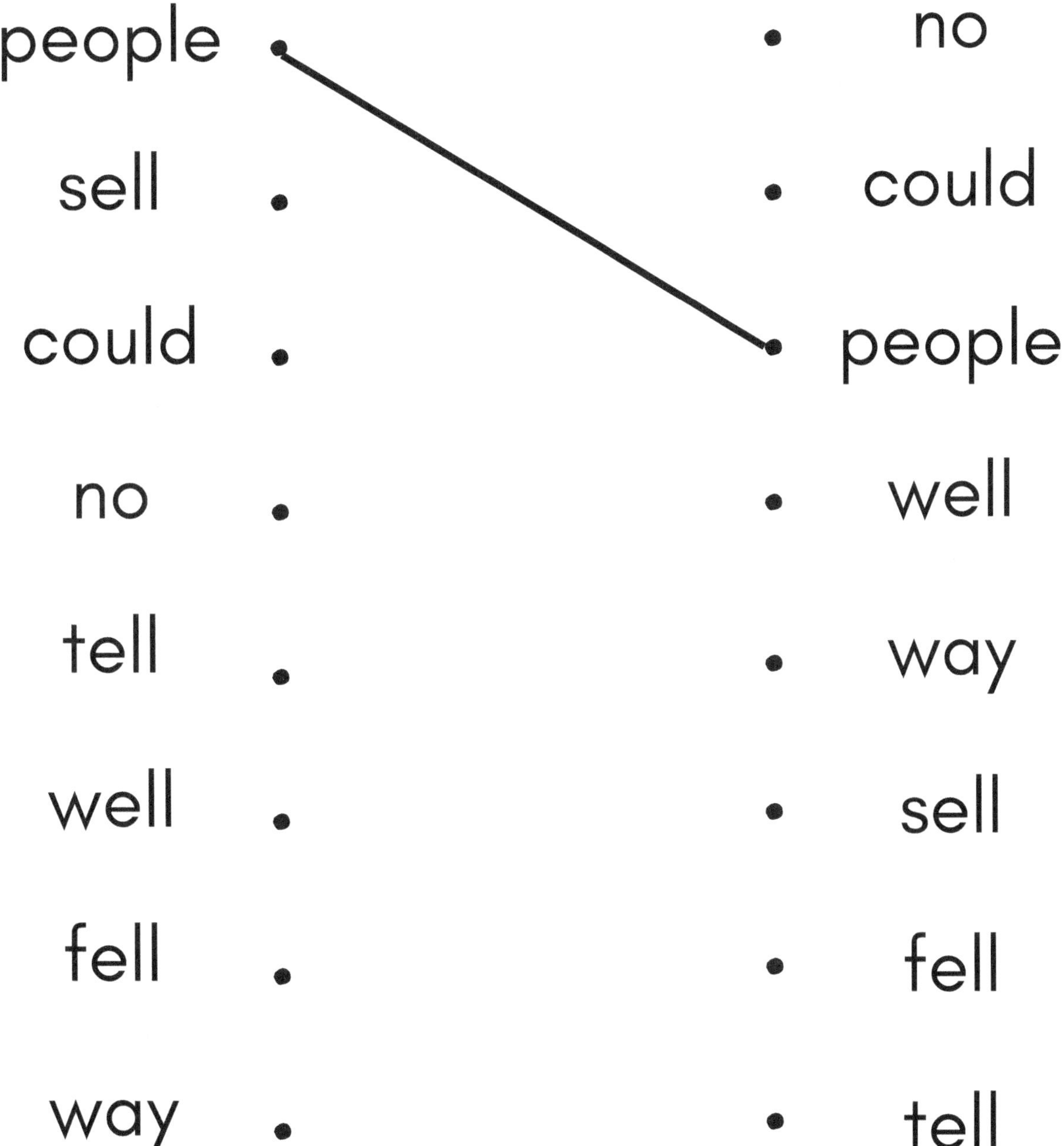

COLORING

Say and color the words.

people

fell

sell

way

could

tell

no

well

TRACE AND WRITE

Say and trace the word.   Write each word (2) two times.

my

than

first

water

bad

hat

mad

glad

FIND THE WORDS

Say the words below. Read the sentences and circle the words.

my	first	water	hat
bad	mad	glad	than

1. I was first in the water.

2. David was glad he was next.

3. I am a better swimmer than David.

4. My sister's hat fell into the water.

5. She was feeling so mad.

6. We all felt bad for her.

FIND THE WORD

Circle the correct word to match each picture.

Read the sentences and circle the words.

my   than   bad

1. He has more than me.

2. How bad was your fall?

3. My dog's name is Spot.

COLORING

Say and color the words.

mad

my

first

than

hat

water

glad

bad

TRACE AND WRITE

Say and trace the word.   Write each word (2) two times.

been

called

who

oil

win

tip

kid

ship

Name:

Class:

MATCHING

Draw a line to match the words.

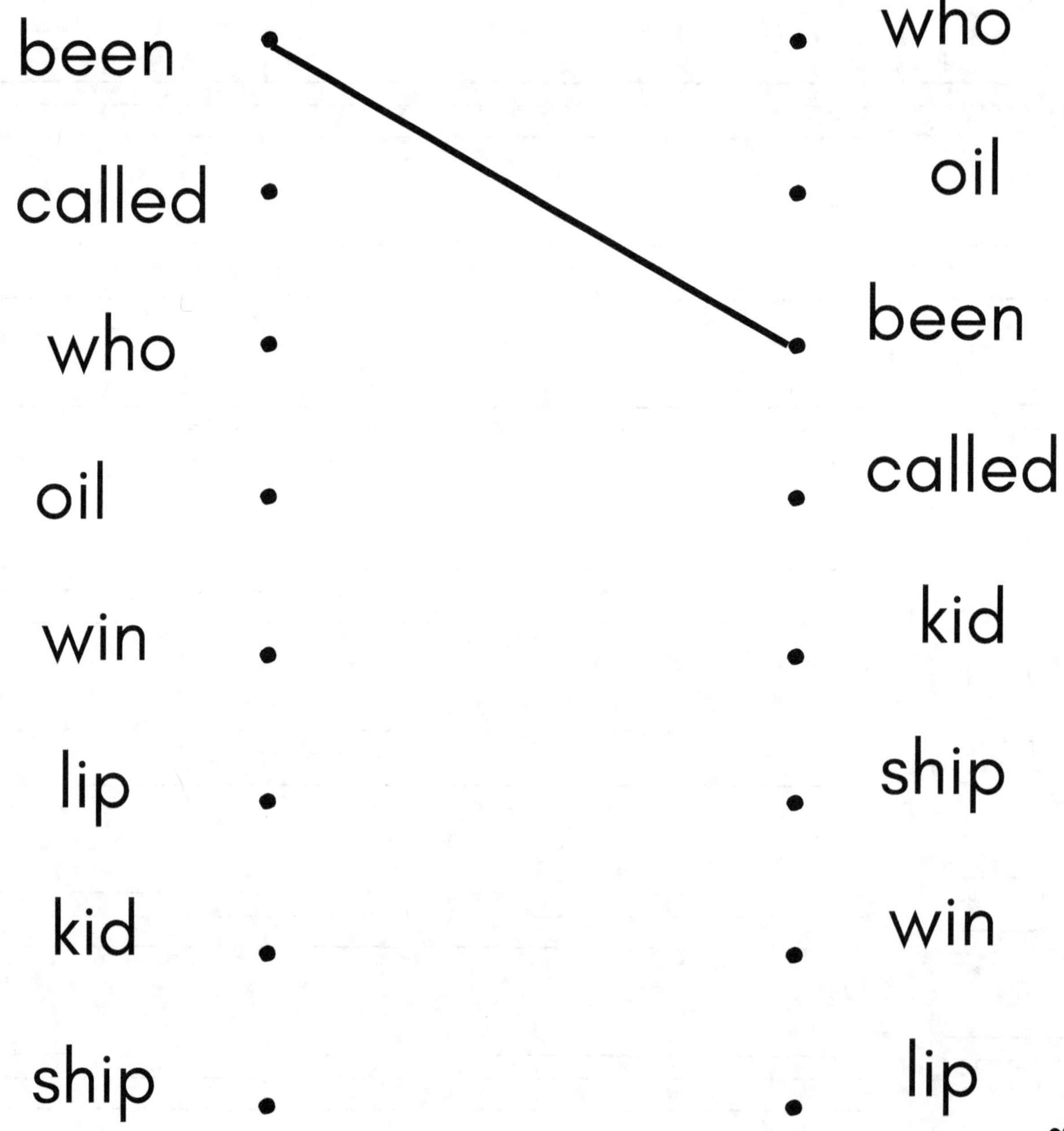

Name:

Class:

WEEK 22

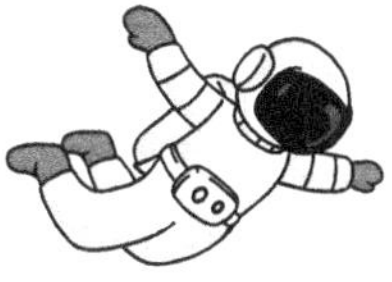

WORD PLANET

Color the planets with the correctly spelled words.

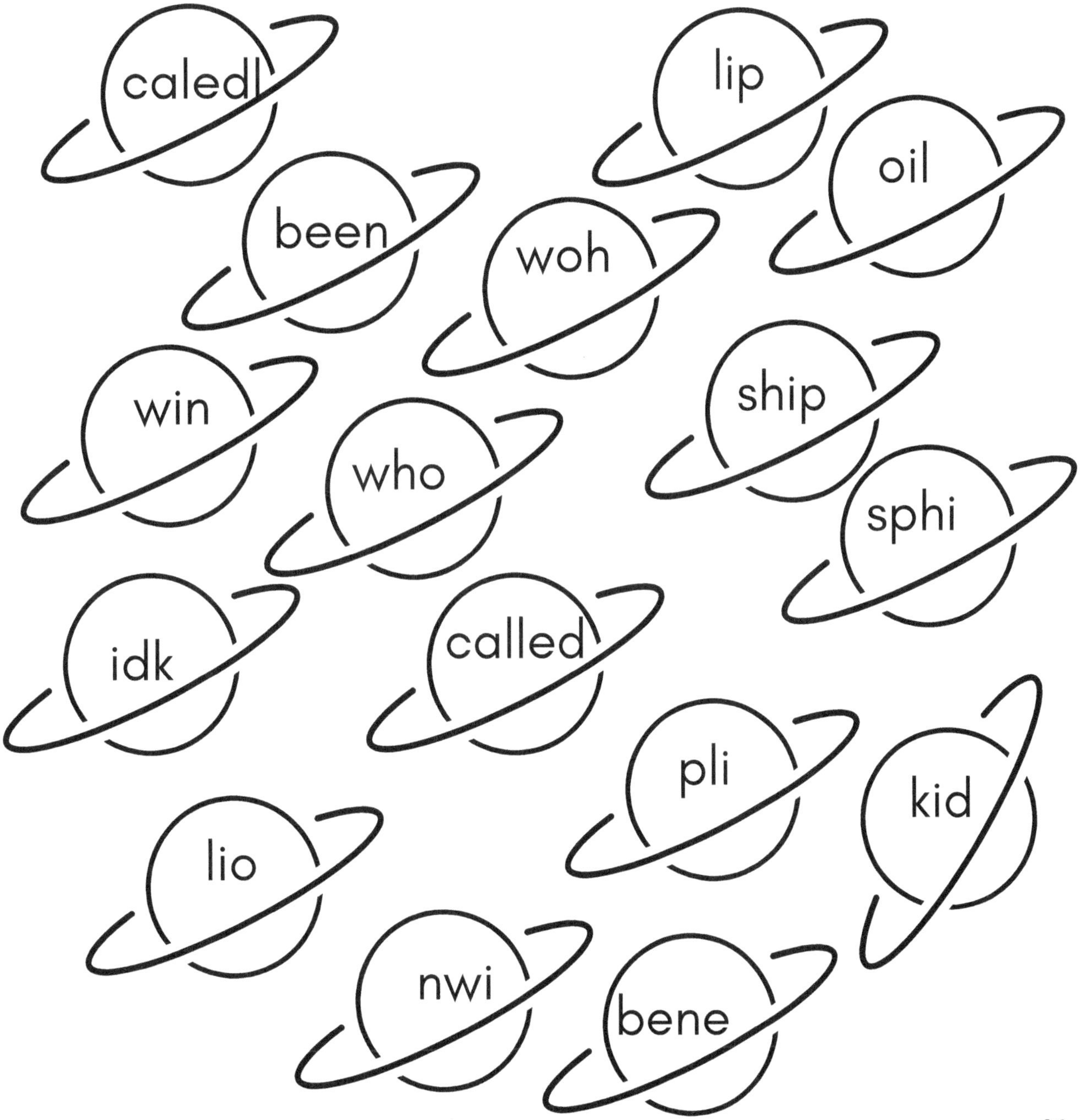

caledl
lip
oil
been
woh
win
ship
who
sphi
idk
called
pli
kid
lio
nwi
bene

COMPLETE THE WORD

Say the words below. Write the missing letter on the blank to complete the word.

been	called	lip	kid
who	oil	win	ship

_alled

_ip

_i_

_hip

_id

_een

_ho

_in

TRACE AND WRITE

Say and trace the word.   Write each word (2) two times.

sit

now

long

mom

fox

chop

shop

find

Name:

Class:

FIND THE WORD

Circle the correctly spelled word to match each picture.

	tis	its	sit
	logn	long	lgon
	mom	mmo	omm
	fxo	fox	ofx
	cpho	chpo	chop
	hsop	shop	oshp
	find	fnid	fidn
	nwo	now	onw

WORD SEARCH

Find and circle the words. Say and check the words that you find.

```
L  S  N  M  O  M  G  S
O  C  H  I  M  V  E  I
N  O  W  C  N  O  W  T
G  C  T  H  E  O  D  R
N  D  G  O  O  F  O  X
S  H  O  P  F  I  N  D
```

shop find chop now

mom fox long sit

COMPLETE THE WORD

Say the words below and write the missing letter on the blank to complete the word.

long	sit	chop	find
mom	fox	shop	now

___hop

___ow

___ind

___ox

___it

___ong

___om

___sho___

TRACE AND WRITE

Say and trace the word.   Write each word (2) two times.

down

day

did

get

bus

truck

must

cut

FIND THE WORD

Circle the correctly spelled word in each set.

dwno	down	wdon
yad	dya	day
ddi	ddi	did
gte	etg	get
bsu	sbu	bus
trcku	truck	ructk
tmus	msut	must
tcu	cut	utc

Name:

Class:

COLORING

Say and color the words.

did

get

bus

truck

down

day

must

cut

MATCHING

Draw a line to match the words.

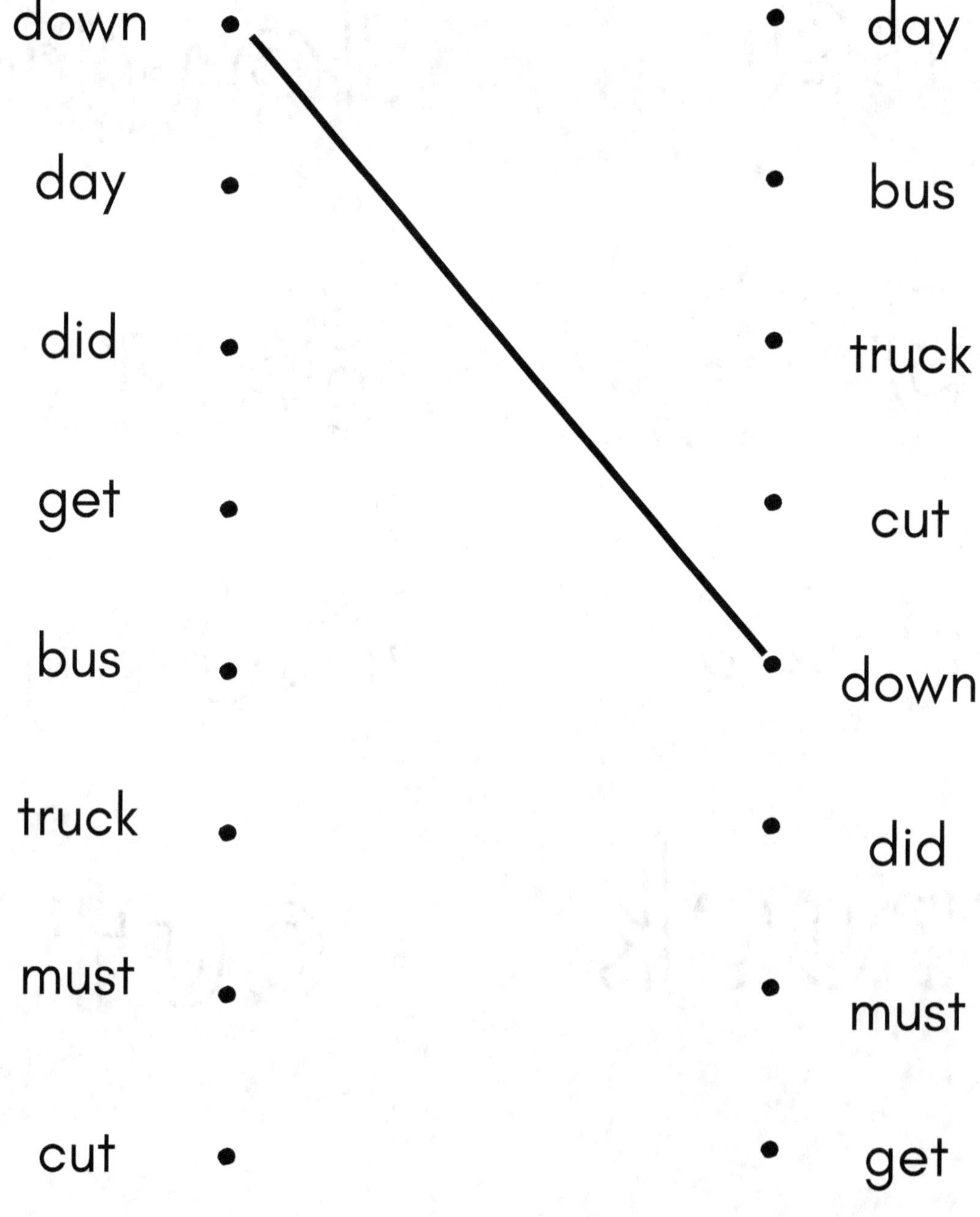

TRACE AND WRITE

Say and trace the word.   Write each word (2) two times.

come

made

may

part

web

tell

less

shell

Name:

Class:

WEEEK 25

BEEHIVE

Find and color the correctly spelled words in the honeycombs.

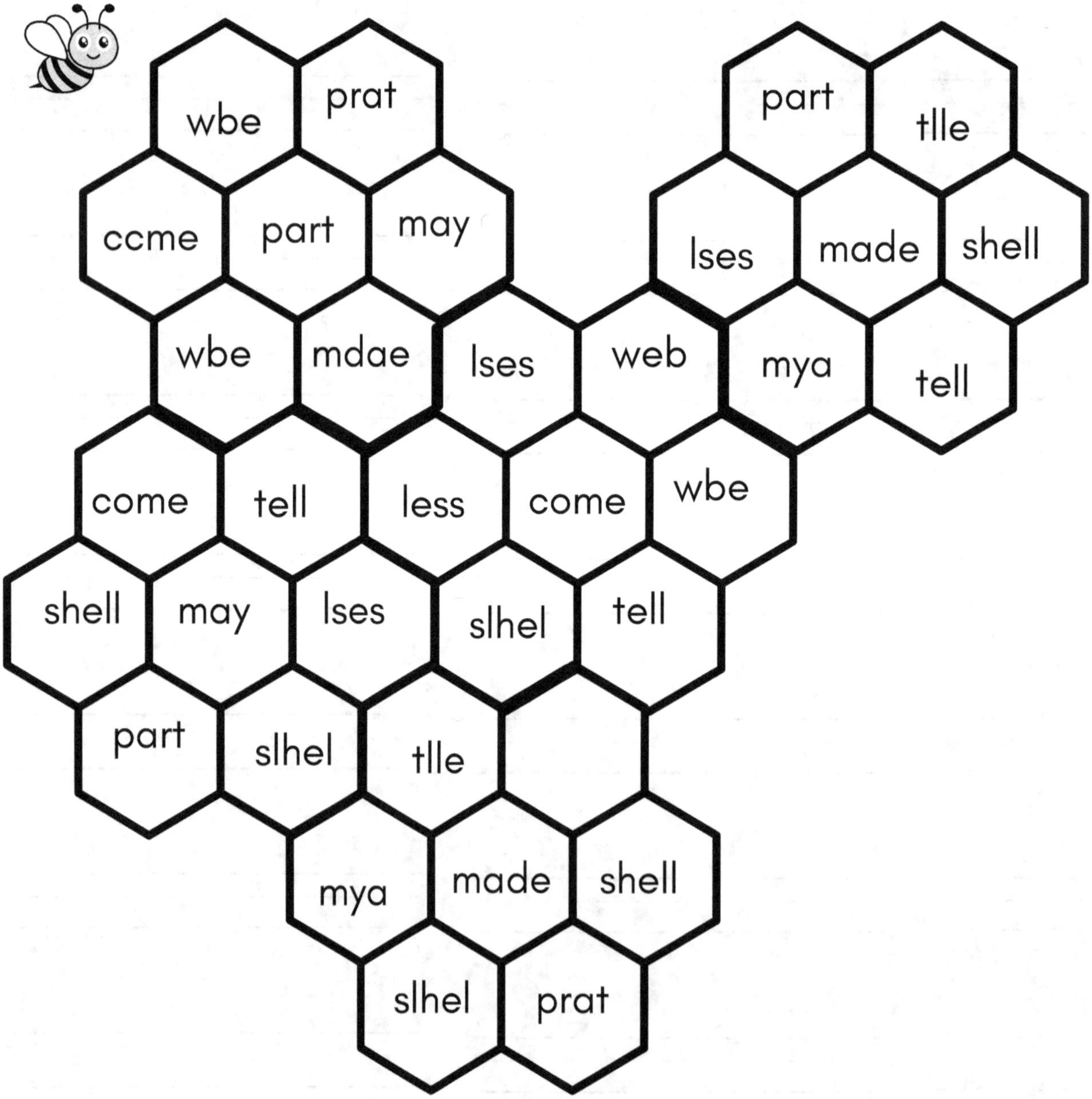
wbe
prat
part
tlle
ccme
part
may
lses
made
shell
wbe
mdae
lses
web
mya
tell
come
tell
less
come
wbe
shell
may
lses
slhel
tell
part
slhel
tlle
mya
made
shell
slhel
prat

CROSS WORD

Follow the numbers and fill in the crossword grid with the correct words.

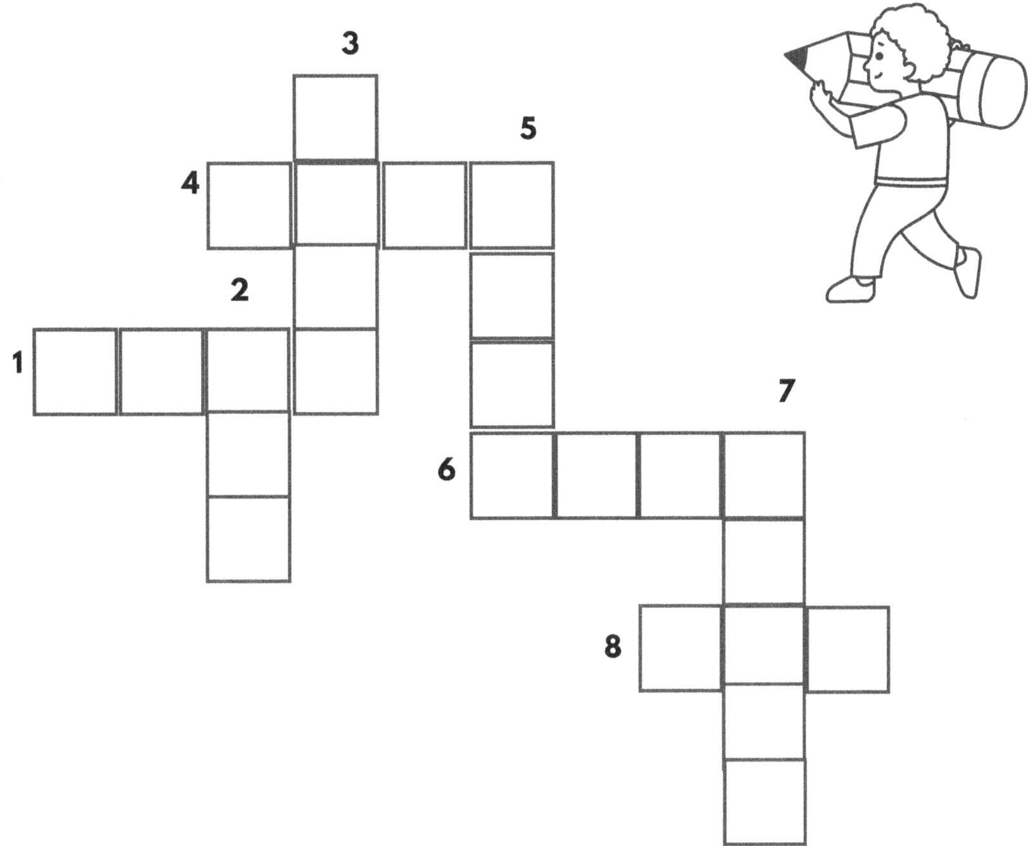

ACROSS

1. come
4. part
5. tell
7. shell

DOWN

2. may
3. made
6. less
8. web

BUILDING A WORD

Draw a line to complete the word.

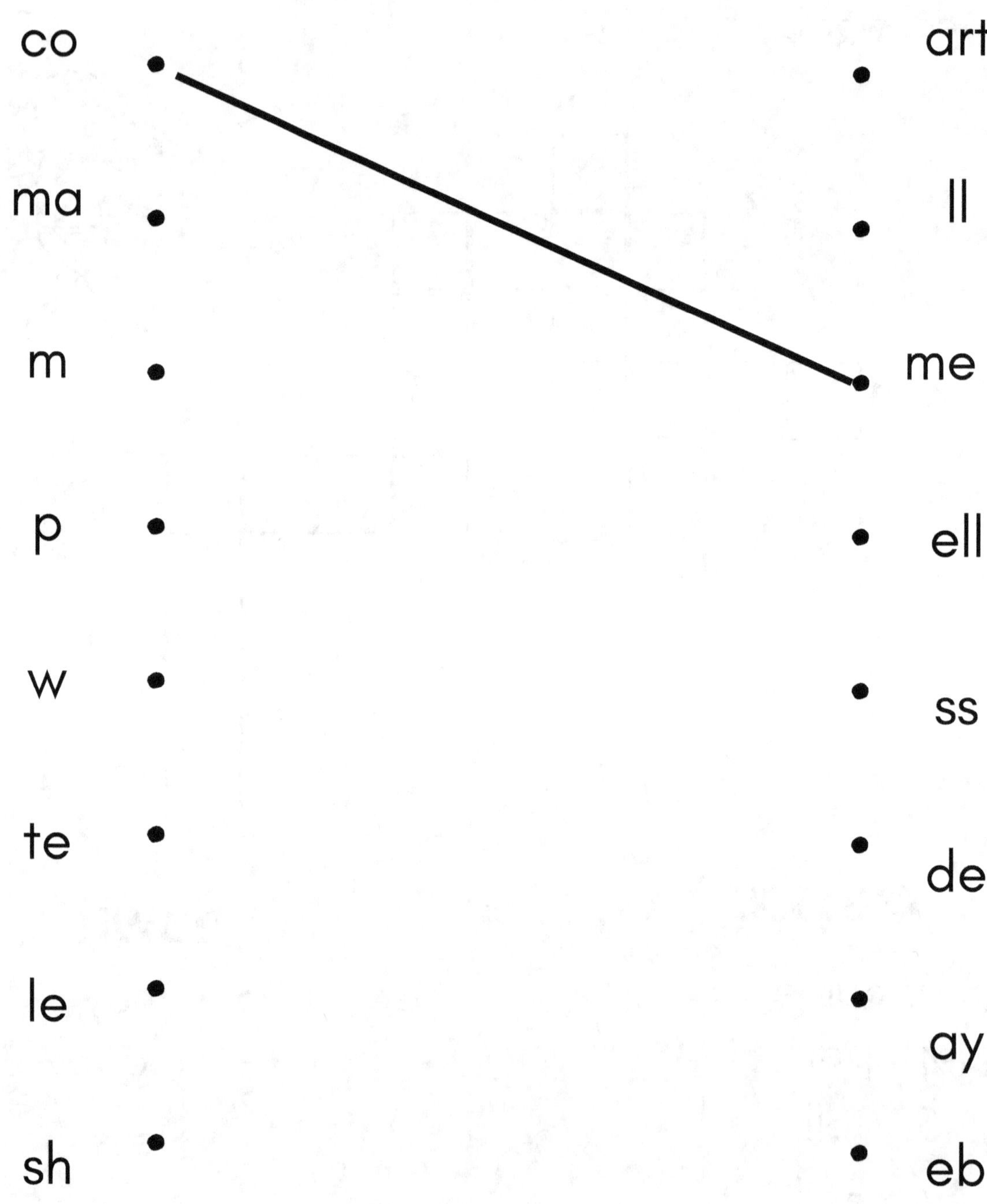

TRACE AND WRITE

Say and trace the word.   Write each word (2) two times.

make

page

race

tape

name

shake

plants

animals

FILL IN THE BLANKS

Look at the pictures below. Say what you see out loud.
What do you hear? Add the missing letter on the blank.

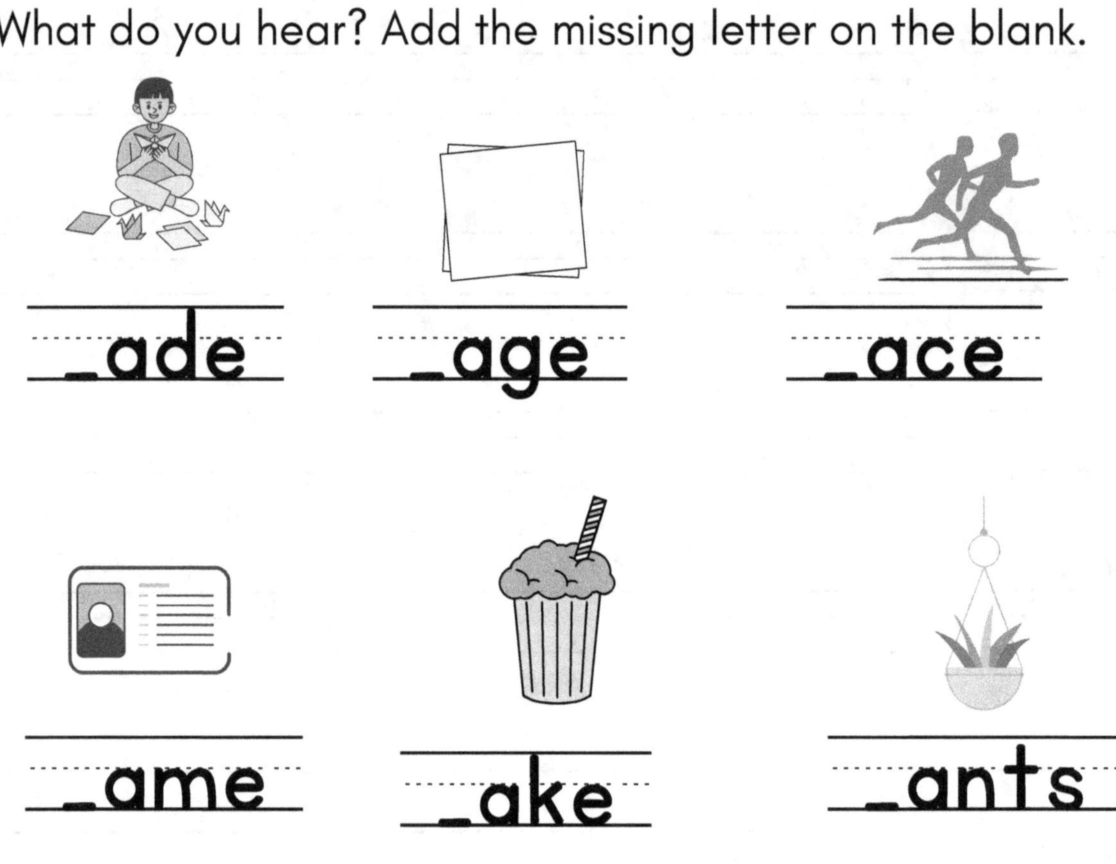

Name:

Class:

WEEK 26

MATCHING

Draw a line to match the word with the correct picture.

shake	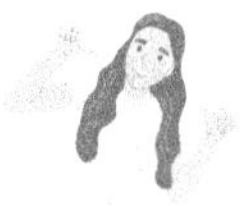
make	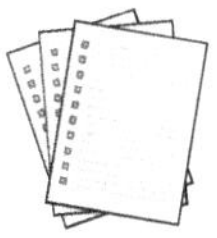
page	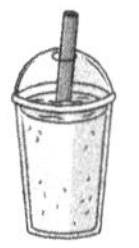
animals	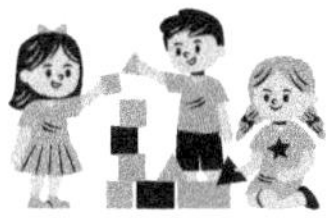
name	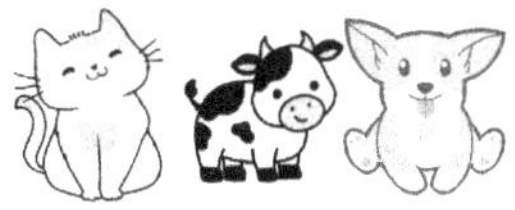
race	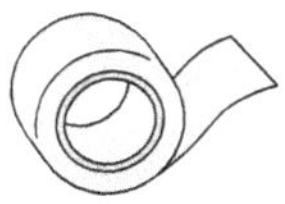
tape	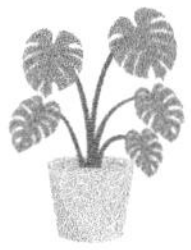
plants	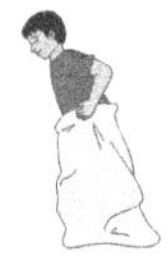

FILL IN THE BLANKS

Look at the pictures below. Say what you see out loud.
What do you hear? Add the missing letter on the blank.

p _ a n t s

m _ k e

p _ g e

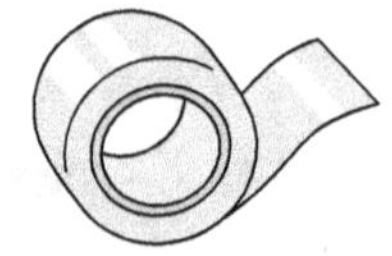
t _ p e

n _ m e

r _ c e

s _ a k e

a _ i m a l s

TRACE AND WRITE

Say and trace the word.   Write each word (2) two times.

way

pay

stay

clay

play

tray

roots

leaves

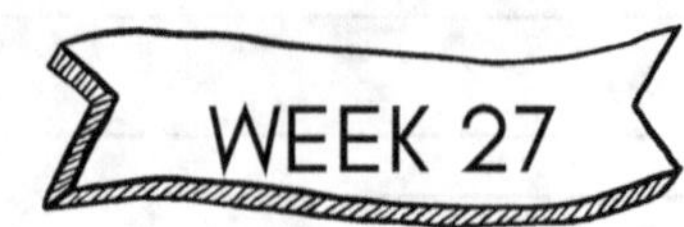

Name:

Class:

WEEK 27

MATCHING

Draw a line to match the word with the correct picture.

way • 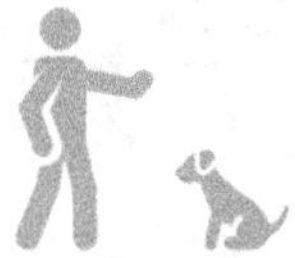

pay • 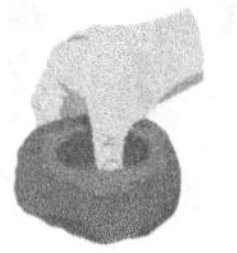

stay • 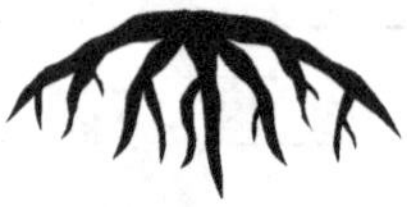

clay • 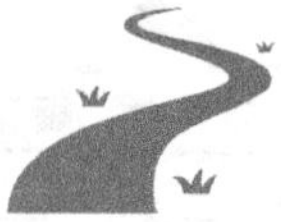

play • 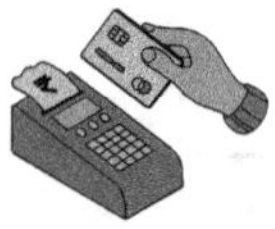

tray • 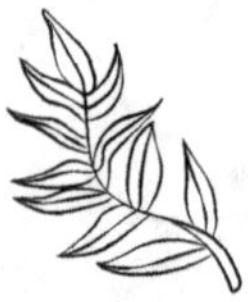

roots • 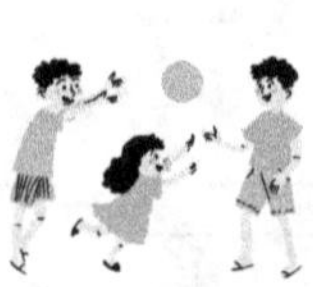

leaves • 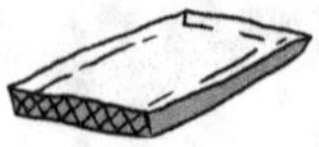

COMPLETE THE WORD

Say the words below and write the missing letter on the blank to complete the word.

| way | leaves | tray | pay |
| play | roots | stay | clay |

w _ y

p _ y

p l _ y

r _ o t s

s t _ y

c l _ y

t r _ y

l _ a v e s

Name:

Class:

WEEK 27

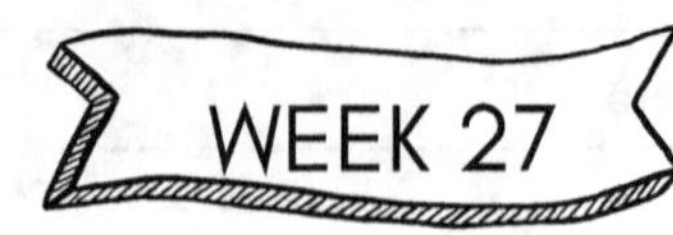

BUILDING A WORD

Draw a line to complete the word.

w •	• lay
p •	• ray
s •	• eaves
c •	• ay
p •	• lay
t •	• tay
r •	• ay
l •	• oots

TRACE AND WRITE

Say and trace the word.   Write each word (2) two times.

nice

drive

mine

wise

dime

five

shelter

nesting

COLORING

Say and color the words.

drive   nice

dime   mine

shelter   wise

five   nesting

DIVING

Help the diver find the words that are spelled corectly.

Circle the correctly spelled words.

diver

nime

ivfe

nice

esnting

wise

isew

drive

shelter

imde

dime

nesting

neic

mine

five

shlteer

WORD SEARCH

Find and circle the words. Say and check the words that you find.

N	I	C	E	I	F	G	H	H	B	L	S
E	S	N	M	I	I	G	A	R	A	G	H
S	C	H	I	M	V	E	Y	F	I	V	E
T	C	A	E	N	E	G	L	D	H	B	L
I	C	T	E	E	G	D	R	I	R	O	T
N	O	O	V	O	S	R	L	M	I	N	E
G	A	I	T	I	C	I	O	E	O	F	R
E	R	D	C	E	T	V	A	O	M	M	D
D	F	I	W	I	S	E	O	O	M	H	T

shelter	dime	drive	mine
nesting	five	wise	nice

TRACE AND WRITE

Say and trace the word.   Write each word (2) two times.

dry

cry

sky

shy

spy

try

tight

soil

FIND THE WORD

Circle the correct word to match each picture.

ryd
dry
dyr

ilght
lihgt
light

tyr
try
rty

ksy
sky
ksy

spy
syp
pys

ycr
rcy
cry

syh
shy
hsy

soil
osil
oils

FILL IN THE BLANKS

Look at the pictures below. Say what you see out loud.
What do you hear? Add the missing letter on the blank.

d _ y

s _ y

s _ y

c _ y

c _ i m b

s _ i l

s _ y

l _ g h t

Name:

Class:

CROSSWORD

Follow the numbers and fill in the crossword grid with the correct words.

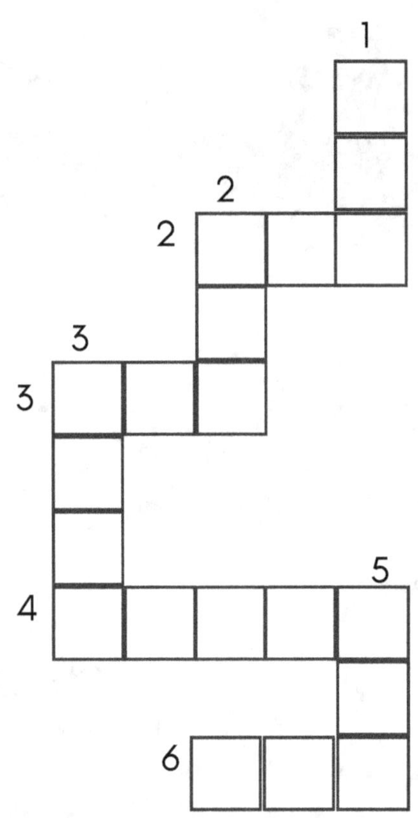

DOWN

1 cry

2 sky

3 soil

5 try

ACROSS

2 shy

3 spy

4 light

6 dry

TRACE AND WRITE

Say and trace the word.   Write each word (2) two times.

nose

bone

code

spoke

hote

note

weather

seasons

FIND THE WORD

Circle the correct word to match each picture.

nsoe
nose
neos

bnoe
bone
bone

code
odce
eodc

spoke
sopke
spoke

tone
tnoe
onte

hloe
hole
lohe

wehtear
weather
weahtre

easonss
seasons
sesoans

Name:

Class:

CROSSWORD

Follow the numbers and fill in the crossword grid with the correct words.

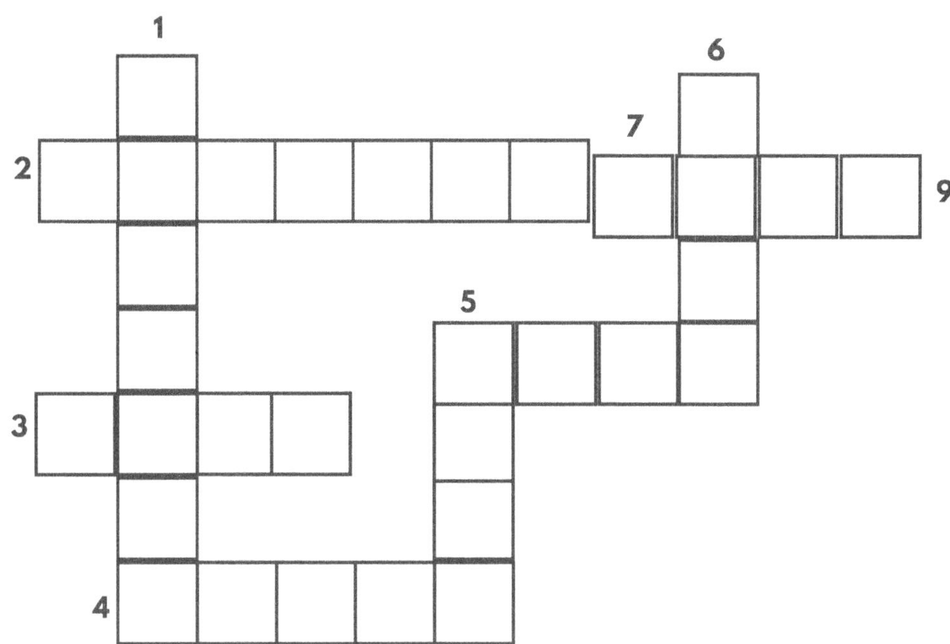

Down

1 seasons

5 nose

6 bone

Across

2 weather

3 code

4 sopke

5 note

7 hole

UNSCRAMBLE

Look at the pictures below. Say what you see out loud. What do you hear? Add the correctly spelled word to the blank.

wetahre ________________

saesnso ________________

nbeo ________________

psoke ________________

otne ________________

helo ________________

seno ________________

deco ________________

TRACE AND WRITE

Say and trace the word.   Write each word (2) two times.

low

snow

grow

flow

show

blow

above

below

Name:

Class:

WEEK 31

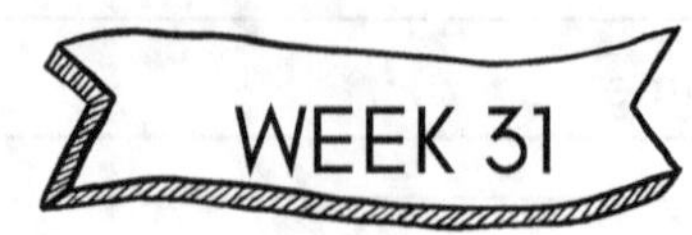

MATCHING

Draw a line to match the word with the correct picture.

low	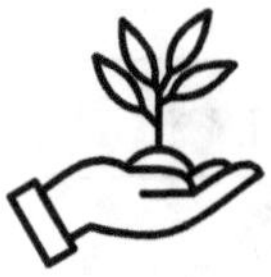
snow	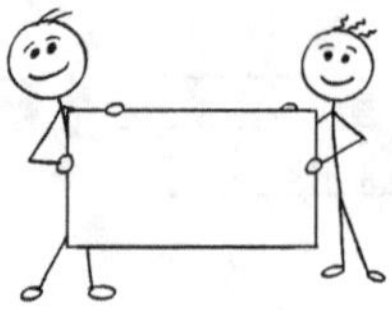
grow	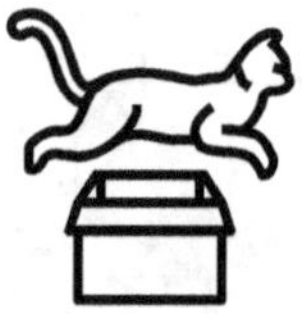
flow	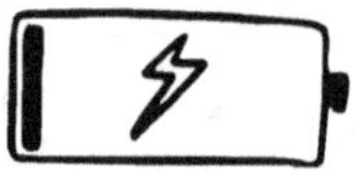
show	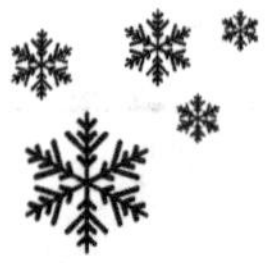
blow	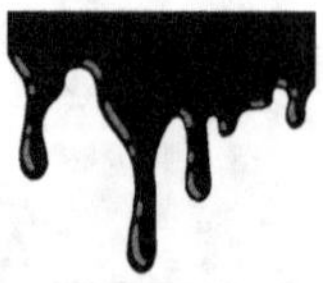
above	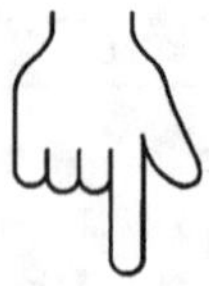
below	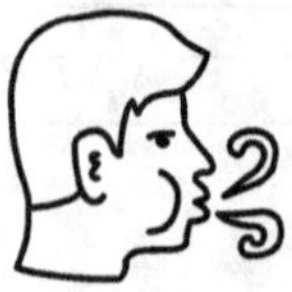

Name:

Class:

WEEK 31

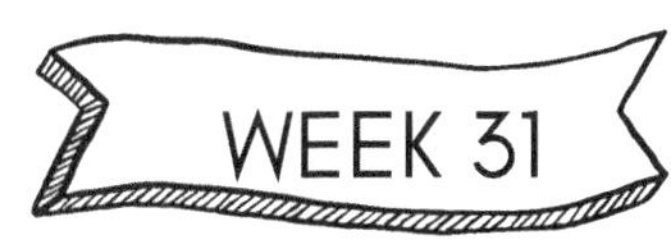

FILL IN THE BLANKS

Look at the pictures below. Say what you see out loud.

What do you hear? Add the missing letter on the blank.

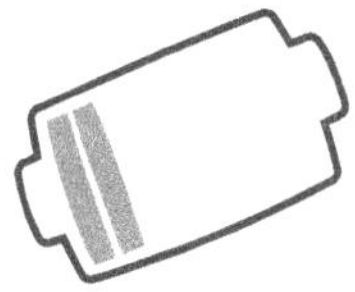

l _ w

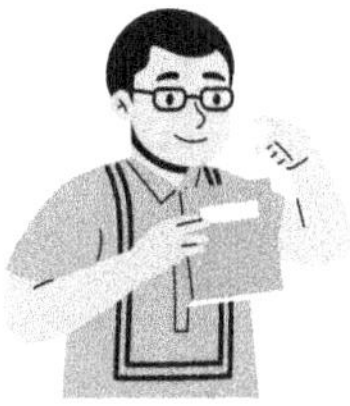

s _ o w

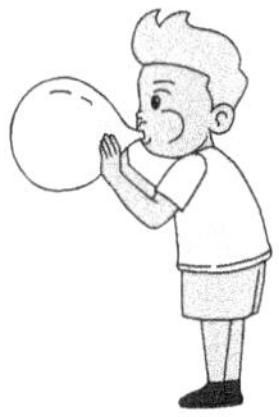

b _ o w

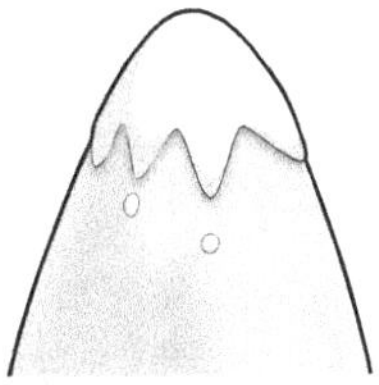

s _ o w

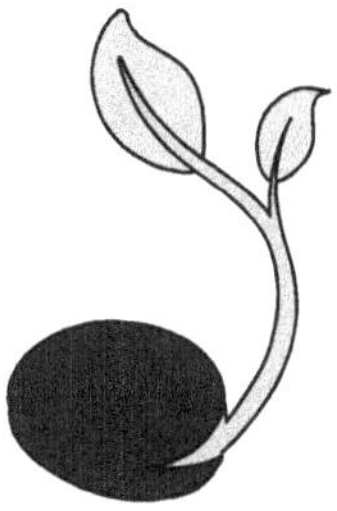

g _ o w

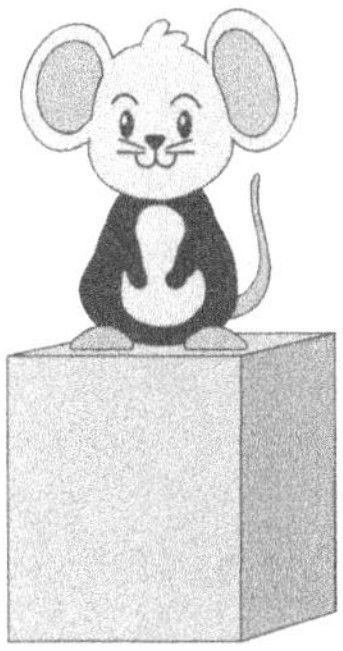

b _ l o w

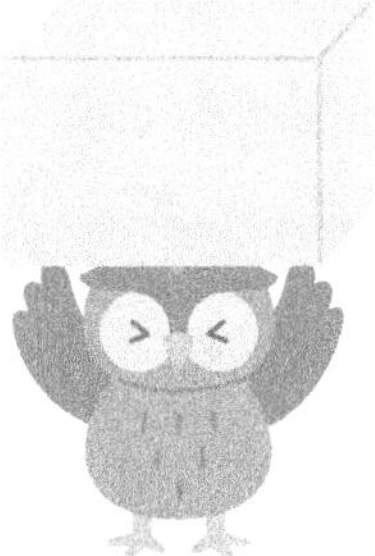

a _ o v e

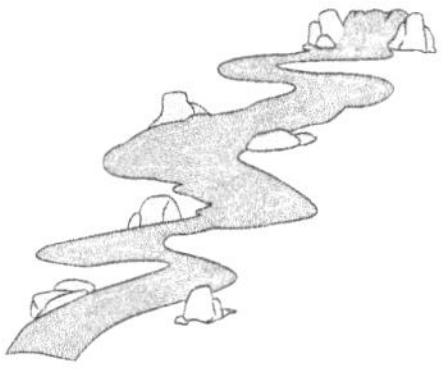

f _ o w

Name:

Class:

CROSSWORD

Follow the numbers and fill in the crossword grid with the correct words.

Down

1 flow

3 below

4 blow

6 show

Across

2 low

5 above

6 snow

7 grow

TRACE AND WRITE

Say and trace the word.   Write each word (2) two times.

coat

boat

float

soak

load

soap

solid

liquid

FILL IN THE BLANKS

Look at the pictures below. Say what you see out loud.
What do you hear? Add the missing letter on the blank.

MATCHING

Draw a line to match the word with the correct picture.

soak

soap

load

liquid

solid

coat

float

boat

BUILD A WORD

Connect the given letters to build the word.

fl	at
co	ap
so	oat
lo	uids
bo	ad
so	lids
so	ak
liq	at

TRACE AND WRITE

Say and trace the word.   Write each word (2) two times.

hook

took

good

stood

wood

look

gas

heated

MATCHING

Draw a line to match the words.

hook	took
took	good
good	hook
stood	stood
wood	heated
look	look
gas	wood
heated	gas

WORD SEARCH

Find and circle the words. Say and check the words that you find.

```
W  L  R  W  A  H  O  M  E  H
G  I  M  O  U  E  E  B  L  O
A  M  P  O  G  A  H  H  B  O
G  O  O  D  E  T  L  O  O  K
A  U  C  H  A  O  E  L  E  O
S  A  G  N  Y  O  I  Z  A  R
E  C  E  B  B  K  R  X  R  T
S  T  O  O  D  T  L  O  H  O
```

wood   hook   gas   good

look   took   heated   stood

FILL IN THE BLANKS

Look at the pictures below. Say what you see out loud.
What do you hear? Add the missing letter on the blank.

TRACE AND WRITE

Say and trace the word.   Write each word (2) two times.

cow

plow

brown

town

clown

tower

citizen

vote

Name:

Class:

CROSSWORD

Follow the numbers and fill in the crossword grid with the correct words.

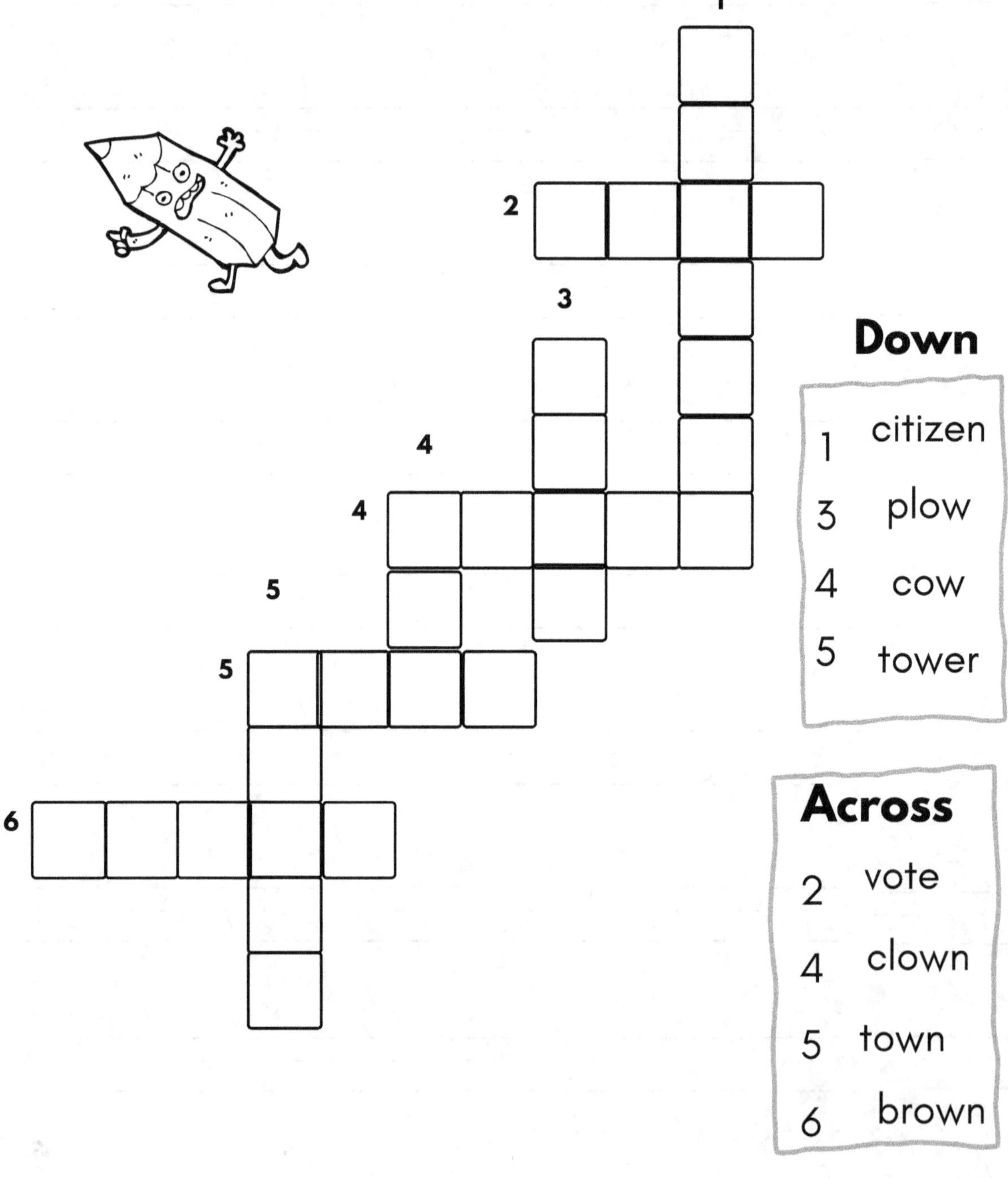

Down

1 citizen

3 plow

4 cow

5 tower

Across

2 vote

4 clown

5 town

6 brown

I CAN SPELL

Look at the pictures below. Say what you see out loud.
What do you hear? Add the missing letter on the blank.

Name:

Class:

FILL IN THE BLANK

Look at the pictures below. Say what you see out loud. What do you hear? Read the sentence and write the correct word on the blank.

1. He has a large ___________________ .

2. We saw a ___________________ bear. 

3. My ___________________ is for Sam. 

4. We saw the tall ___________________ . 

5. I live in a small ___________________ . 

6. We have a ___________________ on our farm. 

7. I am a proud ___________________ . 

8. A ___________________ was at the fair. 

TRACE AND WRITE

Say and trace the word.   Write each word (2) two times.

moon

spoon

tooth

broom

roof

pool

elected

rights

COMPLETE THE WORD

Say the words out loud. What do you hear? Add the missing letter to the blank.

broom	tooth	roof	pool
rights	spoon	moon	elected

r _ g h t s   b r _ o m

t _ o t h   m o _ n

p o _ l   s p _ o n

e l e _ t e d   r _ o f

COLORING

Say and color the words.

spoon   roof

broom   pool

tooth   rights

elected   moon

Name:

Class:

WORD SEARCH

Find and circle the words. Say and check the words that you find.

```
R  I  G  H  T  S  O  T  E  E
O  I  M  O  U  P  E  O  L  L
O  M  O  O  N  O  H  O  B  E
F  O  O  V  E  O  L  T  O  C
A  U  C  H  A  N  E  H  E  T
S  A  M  N  Y  O  I  Z  A  E
E  C  E  B  B  K  R  X  R  D
P  O  O  L  B  R  O  O  M  O
```

spoon   moon   roof   rights

broom   elected   pool   tooth

TRACE AND WRITE

Say and trace the word.   Write each word (2) two times.

deep

feel

green

seed

need

free

globe

symbol

Name:

Class:

CROSSWORD

Follow the numbers and fill in the crossword grid with the correct words.

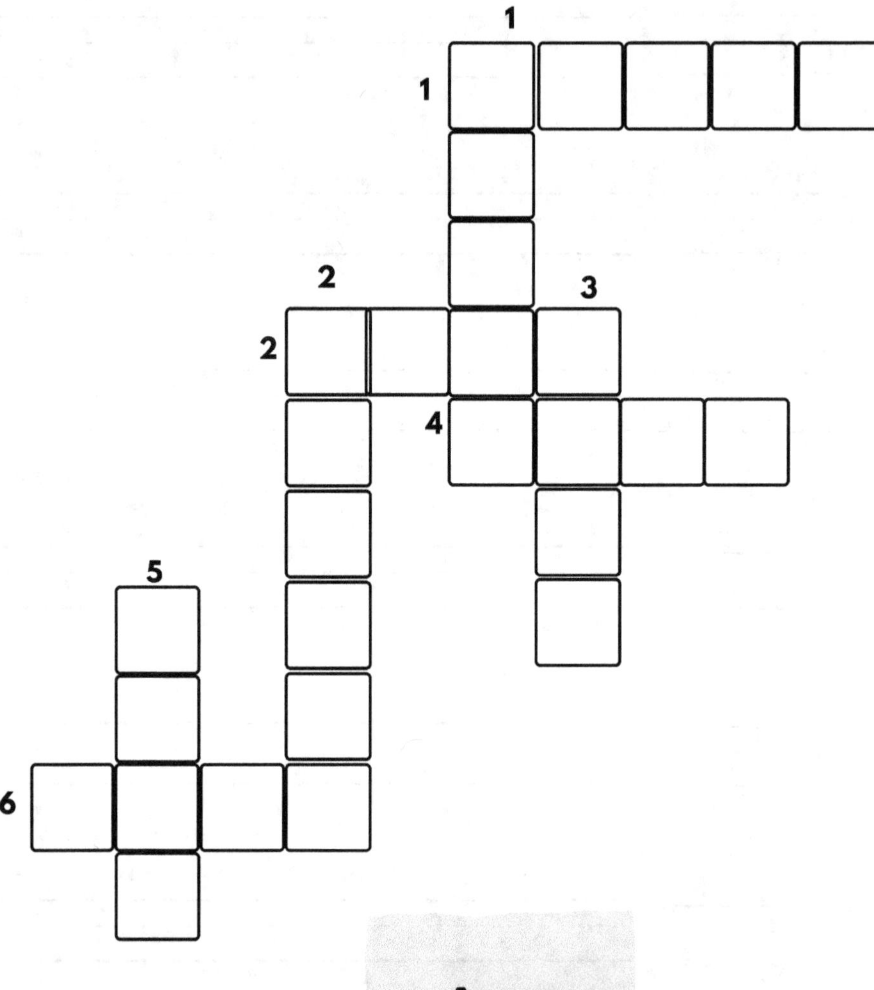

Down

1 green

2 symbol

3 deep

5 free

Across

1 globe

2 seed

4 need

6 feel

COLOR ME

Color all the cirrcles with the correctly spelled words blue.

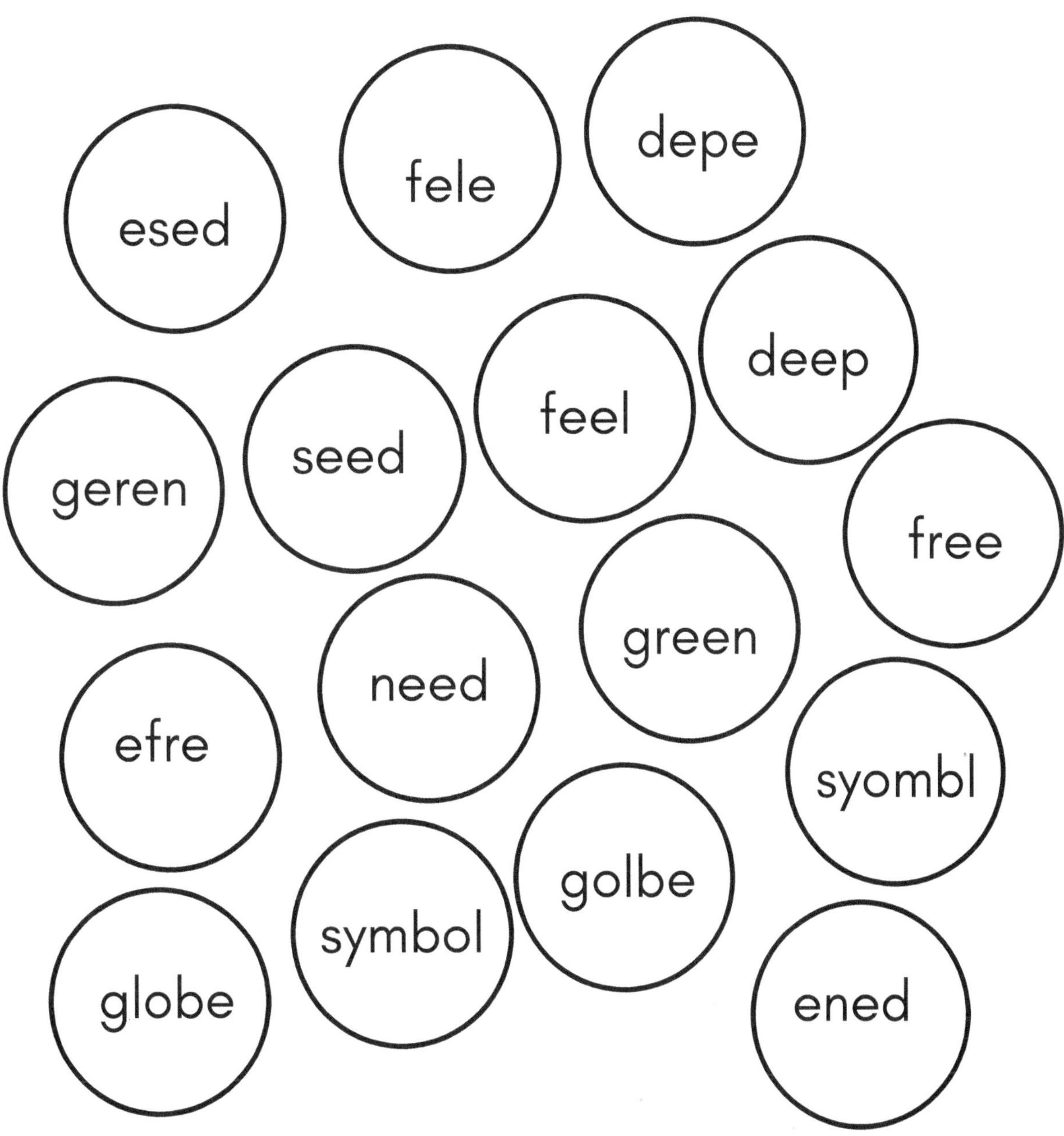

COMPLETE THE SENTENCE

Select the correct word from the list below to complete the sentence.

> need   deep   feel   seed
>
> symbol   globe   green   free

1. A got a _______________ gift.

2. The ship sank in the _______________ sea.

3. The monster is very _______________.

4. I planted a _______________.

5. Do you _______________ help?

6. My teacher has a large _______________.

7. I _______________ great today.

8. The heart is a _______________ of love.

SPELLING WORDS

the	to	that	for	with	at
of	in	it	on	his	be
and	is	he	are	fit	this
a	you	was	as	bit	have
cat	can	map	back	I	big
mat	man	cap	sack	sack	pig
sat	pan	nap	black	they	dig
hat	ran	tap	snack	sit	wig

from	by	what	when	there	which
or	words	all	your	use	she
one	but	were	can	an	do
had	not	we	said	each	how
pin	sick	hot	mop	job	sock
thin	kick	pot	top	mob	rock
spin	brick	not	hop	cob	block
skin	stick	lot	drop	rob	clock

there	other	then	some	like	has
if	about	them	her	into	look
will	out	these	would	time	two
up	many	so	make	him	more
cut	bug	fun	duck	pet	fed
but	hug	sun	luck	get	bed
hut	rug	run	suck	wet	red
shut	mug	bun	stuck	let	sled

write	no	my	been	sit	down
go	way	than	called	now	day
see	could	first	who	long	did
number	people	water	oil	mom	get
men	tell	bad	win	fox	bus
hen	well	hat	lip	chop	truck
ten	sell	mad	kid	shop	must
pen	fell	glad	ship	find	cut

come
made
may
part
web
tell
less
shell

make
page
race
tape
name
shake
plants
animals

way
pay
stay
clay
play
tray
roots
leaves

nice
drive
mine
wise
daime
five
shelter
nesting

dry
cry
sky
shy
spy
try
light
soil

nose
bone
code
spoke
hole
note
weather
seasons

low
snow
grow
flow
show
blow
above
below

coat
boat
float
soak
load
soap
solid
liquid

hook
took
good
stood
wood
look
gas
heated

cow
plow
brown
town
clown
tower
citizen
vote

moon
spoon
tooth
broom
roof
pool
elected
rights

deep
feel
green
seed
need
free
globe
symbol

Wow, you're now a proud owner of our book! We hope you've been whisked away on a thrilling journey! If you've got a moment to spare, scan the QR code below and leave us a review. Your thoughts are like gold to us and help us spread the word about our incredible books!

CERTIFICATE OF COMPLETION

Presented to

____

For completing the

1st Grade Spelling Workbook

YOU'RE A CHAMP!